WO

LEARNING &

DEVELOPMENT

I would like to dedicate this book to the memory of my uncle, Neil Clive Tilbury. Thank you to my loving and supportive parents, Claire and Peter, and of course my ever-patient husband, Majid.

Jackie

This book is dedicated to my father, George Thorpe 1924–2005. And also to his grandchildren, Daniel and Emily.

Sara

WORKPLACE LEARNING & DEVELOPMENT

Delivering Competitive Advantage for Your Organization

Jackie Clifford
& Sara Thorpe

KOGAN PAGE

London and Philadelphia

First published in Great Britain and the United States in 2007 by Kogan Page Limited

First South Asian Edition 2007

120 Pentonville Road
London N1 9JN
United Kingdom
www.kogan-page.co.uk

4737/23, Ansari Road
Daryaganj, New Delhi-110 002
India
www.vivagroupindia.net

ISBN 10: 0 7494 5152 1
ISBN 13: 978 0 7494 5152 3

British Library Cataloguing-in-Publication Data

A CIP record for this book is available from the British Library.

Library of Congress Cataloging-in-Publication Data

Clifford, Jackie.
Workplace learning and development : delivering competitive advantage for your organizations / Jackie Clifford and Sara Thorpe.
p. cm.
Includes bibliographical references and index.
ISBN-13: 978 0 7494 5152 3
ISBN-10: 0 7494 5152 1
1. Organizational learning. 2. Adult learning. 3. Blended learning. 4. Organizational change. I. Thorpe, Sara. II. Title.
HD58.82.C55 2007
658.3'124–dc22 2006033745

Typesetting by JS Typesetting Ltd., Porthcawl, Mid Glamorgan
Printed and bound in India by Gopsons Papers Ltd., Noida, UP, India.

Contents

	Acknowledgements	*ix*
	Introduction	1
1	**Setting the Scene: Learning and Development in Context**	**5**
	The move from training and development to learning and development	5
	Vocabulary and terminology – what do we mean?	7
2	**Analysing Development Needs**	**11**
	Identifying the impact of changes	12
	Clarifying standards	12
	Assessing the current position	13
3	**An Introduction to Adult Learning**	**19**
	Knowledge, skills and attitudes – Bloom's taxonomy	19
	Kolb's experiential learning cycle	20
	Honey and Mumford's learning styles	21
	Sensory learning preferences	22
	Theory of competence	23
	Motivating adults to learn	26
	Organizational learning	27
4	**Learning and Development Methods**	**29**
	Action learning	29
	Apprenticeships	33

	Coaching	36
	Delegation	39
	Discussion boards and groups	43
	Distance learning	45
	Drama-based learning	48
	E-learning	52
	Executive coaching	58
	Mentoring	60
	Networking	63
	On-the-job training	67
	Outdoor education/learning	70
	Professional membership	74
	Professional supervision	77
	Projects	79
	Qualifications	82
	Case study: NVQ level 4 in management of learning and development provision	89
	Reflective practice	92
	Secondments	96
	Self-study	99
	Shadowing	102
	Temporary promotion	105
	Trade exhibitions	107
	Training courses	109
	Organizational learning methods	116
5	**Selecting the Right Methods**	**119**
	Checklist for selecting development methods	119
	Girlguiding UK – competency-based learning development case study	129
6	**Development Plans: Theory into Practice**	**133**
	Development plans	133
	Case study 1: Absence management skills at Three Valleys Water Ltd	137
	Case study 2: Meeting the development needs of a small business	140
	Case study 3: Multi-skilling call centre agents	142
	Case study 4: Using NVQs as a team development tool	144
	Case study 5: Two approaches to the development of time management skills	147

	Case study 6: Personal development to improve leadership skills	151
	Case study 7: Manager as researcher	153
7	**Assessing the Impact**	**157**
	Why assess the impact?	157
	How can the impact be assessed?	158
	Added value and unintended outcomes	163
8	**Putting Your Learning into Practice**	**167**
	References and Further Reading	*169*
	Index	*175*

Acknowledgements

We thank all the people who have supported and encouraged us during the writing of this book and particularly those who have contributed case studies and information.

Introduction

The purpose of this book is to explore alternative learning methods and ways of developing individuals that provide flexible approaches and support trainer-led courses.

Throughout this book we are addressing 'you', assuming that you have responsibility for the development of others and yourself, whatever your job title or role within the organization. We focus on workplace development, meaning development that takes place within organizations, whether that organization is private, not-for-profit or public sector and whether its members are paid or unpaid.

Our aim is to help you maximize the returns you get by investing in development, which we believe can only happen by using a variety of different methods. Large amounts of time and money are invested in training courses, but organizations fail to realize that simply providing a course can take individuals only so far. Training courses are an excellent way to give learners new skills, knowledge and techniques; however, to improve performance the learning must be embedded and transferred to the workplace. To impact performance effectively, organizations must maximize the skills, knowledge and behaviours available to them, which means that they need to ensure individuals are learning, not just new skills and knowledge, but also how to use the ones they have more effectively and in new situations along with learning how to learn.

The core beliefs upon which this book is based are:

- Training courses do work, but are not the answer to all development and learning needs. See the section on training courses.
- There are many different learning and development methods, all of which are equally valid; however, some are not suitable for a specific person or situation.

- Learning and development is increasingly accepted as being the responsibility of individuals and their line managers who need to know what is available to them and how to use it in a development context.
- Traditionally, training courses were seen as the way of teaching or educating within the workplace. It is well documented that times have changed and focus is increasingly on more flexible approaches to achieving learning and development.
- The key to successful development is selecting the right method at the right time.
- Learning and development is essential to organizational success. The current pace of change means that everyone must continue to develop in order simply to stay in the same place and even more so to 'keep ahead of the game'.
- Every individual has the capacity to learn and develop, regardless of their background, capabilities or current level of knowledge and skill.
- Learning and development does not necessarily need to be expensive. It does involve an investment – of time and/or money – but does not necessarily need to cost thousands of pounds.

By using this book, you will be able to:

- identify a range of different methods that will help individuals to learn;
- select methods appropriate to different situations and in doing so utilize your resources wisely;
- develop high-quality learning programmes for individuals and your organization;
- measure the impact of development on your organization.

If you are simply in the business of ticking a box to say that you have provided 200 hours worth of training for your staff, don't read this book! This book is about truly making a difference through learning and development – it is about contributing to your 'business' by changing or increasing people's skills, knowledge and behaviours.

Read this book if you are interested in finding out more about flexible learning strategies. We begin by setting the scene and discussing the context of learning and development in the 21st century. We go on to offer you information about the different learning and development methods that people talk about (and a few they don't!), why you might use them and how to make them work. You will then have the opportunity to reflect on the decision-making process – how do you select the right method for your particular situation? Helpful in this decision-making process may be our examples of how others have used some of these development methods and some ideas of how they could be used to address specific needs. Finally comes evaluation and assessing the impact of the chosen methods.

1

Setting the Scene: Learning and Development in Context

Fundamentally employees have five questions which they require the organization to answer in order to perform effectively:

1 What do you want me to do?
2 How do you want me to do it?
3 How are you going to measure my success and performance?
4 How am I doing?
5 Where can I go from here?

Figure 1.1 illustrates how learning and development maps onto these five questions and onto people management processes in general. This diagram shows that workplace development is an integral part of performance management, business improvement and individual well-being.

THE MOVE FROM TRAINING AND DEVELOPMENT TO LEARNING AND DEVELOPMENT

Organizations have always needed to have good people who can perform effectively in their job; this is increasingly important as the pace of change becomes more rapid. Here is the conflict: budgets are tighter, organizations

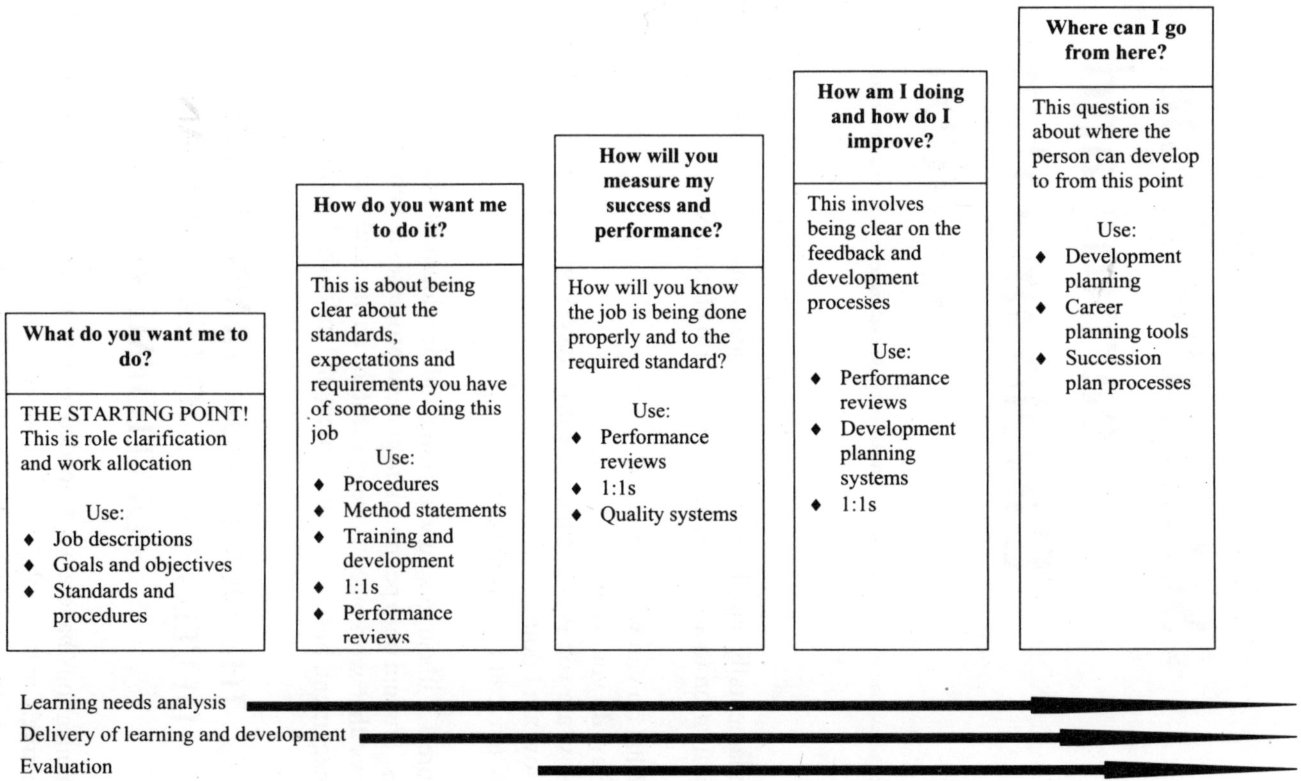

Figure 1.1 The organizational context of workplace development

are smaller, which means that people have less money and time to spend on training and development. Yet the nature of today's world means that organizations actually have more development needs and requirements. Our world is different: we have technology that even a few years ago was sci-fi, globalization is affecting structures and cultures, legislation is impacting all working practices, and individuals have higher expectations of their employers and working lives. In the workplace, employees are required to adapt and respond to these changes quickly and without loss of productivity – this may mean that they have to take on new work, adapt to new processes, receive additional responsibilities, master new technologies and adhere to new legal requirements such as Health and Safety rules and data protection.

Learning needs to be continuous because of the pace of change and therefore it can no longer be the sole responsibility of the HR or training department; individuals and their line managers must be involved and take the lion's share of identifying learning needs and ensuring everyone is appropriately developed to achieve business goals and objectives. Training courses, which were traditionally seen as the way of teaching or educating within the workplace, are no longer sufficient or appropriate for delivering ongoing learning and development.

VOCABULARY AND TERMINOLOGY – WHAT DO WE MEAN?

This may be a good place to clarify what we mean by 'learning', 'training' and 'development'. We have chosen definitions that describe our understanding of a number of terms that will be used throughout this book so that you are aware of our perspective. Our research came up with many definitions, especially of the word 'learning' – indeed, having agreed definitions is part of the challenge our profession is facing. We would encourage you to explore different authors so that you can achieve your own understanding and/or participate in the debate.

Training is:

> *'An instructor-led, content-based intervention leading to desired changes in behaviour.'* (Sloman, 2005)

Learning is:

> *'The process of increasing knowledge and skills and developing our attitudes or beliefs so that we have the opportunity for*

increased choice' (Thorpe and Clifford, 2000). Alan Mumford, in his book Effective Learning *(1995), states that 'learning has happened when people can demonstrate that they know something that they did not know before (insights and realizations as well as facts) and/or when they can do something they couldn't do before (skills).'*

Development is:

The process of growth and learning, resulting in change or progression.

Learning and development is:

A term that is now widely used because the focus has shifted from the person delivering the training to the learner and the impact of learning upon their performance. There is a movement away from the delivery of content to the development of learning capabilities, hence the responsibility being given to the individual and their line manager. A training and development function is more likely to be seen as the central point from which all staff development activity comes, where a learning and development function can be more readily perceived in a consultancy/advisory/facilitatory capacity. Training is one method, out of many, for achieving learning.

Therefore, the learning and development methods explored in Chapter 4 are techniques which can be used to learn knowledge, skills or behaviours and in doing so develop.

A development need is:

The gap between current and required (or desired) performance, which can be filled by learning. In broad terms, there are two types of development need. The first is that which arises from a change – internal or external to the organization. The second is that which arises as a result of reviewing current performance against standards.

Broadly there are three factors that will create a development need:

1. Imposed change: change that happens within an organization (whether internally or externally driven) and leads to a need for different skills, knowledge and behaviours to be demonstrated.

2 Performance review: development needs that arise as a result of reviewing current performance against standards and results (actual or desired). This could be a review that occurs with another person such as your manager or coach, or a self-review process.
3 Personal motivation: when an individual decides to enhance their knowledge and skills or alter their behaviour in order to achieve personal goals, which may be to achieve a promotion, take on a different career, increase their happiness or make other significant life changes.

For the majority of organizations the first two factors will take priority in terms of workplace development and this is appropriate because organizations should be concerned, first and foremost, with achieving their work and business plans. Personally motivated development can be valuable to human resource retention and motivation, but will principally always be 'nice to have' and, when used, should still have some linkages to the business plan or tangible business benefit.

2

Analysing Development Needs

Learning and development within organizations is not going to be delivered unless there is a development need. This might seem like stating the obvious; however, there are many occasions where development activities are requested or arranged, but the need is a disciplinary issue (either the person is not capable or is unwilling to do the job), a process issue (the process is wrong and needs to be changed) or an equipment issue (the equipment is outdated and not fit for purpose).

A development need is where the person will be able to perform the task to the required standard given appropriate time and resource – they have the capability, but they lack the knowledge, skills or behavioural techniques to be able to do it to the required standard *at this time*.

Our fundamental view is that all individuals have the capacity to learn, given sufficient time and support. However, within the workplace, the time and support available are not infinite and therefore it may be necessary to state that someone is 'incapable' of developing to the required standard if they have not achieved this standard after the appropriate learning and development opportunities have been provided. In other words, it is impossible for organizations to invest continually in one person's development without seeing the return on that investment. There are two different types of incapability: the first is due to an inherent incapacity to function, and the second is where an individual fails to achieve owing to their own unwillingness or lack of commitment to the task at hand. Neither of these can be dealt with via development – although this must be offered before you can judge someone to be incapable and to comply with employment law.

So how do you know if a development need exists? The first step is to identify the impact of a change and/or clarify what the required standard of performance is.

IDENTIFYING THE IMPACT OF CHANGES

There are three questions that enable you to assess the impact of a change from a learning and development perspective:

1 Does the change mean that people have to do something differently that requires them to learn new knowledge, skills or behaviours?
2 Would developing individuals/teams help or support change to be more effectively implemented?
3 Will the change result in standards being altered?

CLARIFYING STANDARDS

A standard is the way we expect something to be done, and in order to identify a development need, it is important to be clear about what the required standard is, so that any shortfall can be recognized. In organizations, performance expectations are defined in the following ways:

- industry standards;
- national standards;
- competency schemes;
- job descriptions and specifications;
- value statements;
- method statements;
- systems of work;
- professional standards;
- best practice guidelines;
- stakeholder expectations;
- line managers' expectations;
- quality standards, eg ISO;
- internal and external benchmarks.

Although standards are often drawn from the same sources, they will be unique to an organization because they will have that organization's, and often the line manager's, 'stamp' or interpretation on them. Line managers will often have their own expectations or standards based upon their own experiences – do not discount these, but equally be wary of assuming that they are correct. This is where activities such as benchmarking are useful as they enable you to compare what you are doing with others inside and outside the organization who are doing similar things. Whatever the source of the standards or expectations, they need to be communicated if they are to be met.

Having identified the sources of the standards for the various jobs within the organization, you can gain clarification for the individuals who are doing the jobs by completing the following statement: 'In this organization at this time, this task will be performed correctly/well when....'

For example, our expectations for a receptionist to our business include:

- compliant with the organization's dress code;
- clean, tidy and well groomed;
- greets all visitors with a smile and acknowledgement if dealing with someone else or taking a phone call;
- answers phone calls within three rings and with the format 'Good morning/afternoon, (company name) (receptionist's name), how may I help you?';
- focuses on the visitor – discontinuing any personal conversations with other people for the duration of the interaction;
- offers refreshments and reading material, if the visitor is required to wait;
- offers information where appropriate;
- is at their desk on time and ready to work, at least five minutes before the business day begins;
- ensures that reception is not left unattended.

Once clarified, standards will need to be reviewed and where appropriate updated to make sure that they are in line with current practices and thinking.

The next step is to find out where the gaps exist....

ASSESSING THE CURRENT POSITION

Having identified the desired position, you cannot develop people to reach that position until you know their starting point – where are we in relation to where we want to be? It is rare that a group of individuals trying to develop the same knowledge or skill will have exactly the same starting point; all will have their own past experiences and prior learning upon which to draw. Good learning needs analysis is about identifying the true needs, ie the distance that every individual needs to travel to reach the desired end point.

There are several methods or tools that can be used to help you assess this.

Questionnaires

Often used on an individual level to identify gaps in a specific knowledge or skill area, but they can be used to gather general information about overall learning and development needs. The onus is on the learner to answer honestly and comment on their abilities to do specific jobs. Questionnaires are more useful if they are completed by the learner in conjunction with their line manager or a third party – this supports the learner to be more honest in identifying their areas for development.

In constructing a questionnaire you will be more successful in identifying the real learning needs if you break down the job, task or activity into its component parts and then ask questions about each part. It may be useful to involve a subject expert in writing the questionnaire; however, be aware that technical experts will often use language that the learners cannot relate to.

One of the drawbacks of questionnaires is that learners may not be able to answer them fully because they are at the unconscious incompetence stage; they don't know what they don't know and therefore, if the questions are not specific enough, the learner will not be able to provide accurate information about their needs.

Wherever possible, use a pilot for your questionnaire – this enables you to consider whether you are getting the type of answers that you are looking for and, if not, will allow you to revise the questionnaire prior to full circulation.

Interviews

This could be the recruitment interview or a 1:1 interview with an existing staff member. In a structured interview, individuals are asked a set list of questions from which there is little deviation. This takes less time to conduct and analyse than an unstructured interview. However, an unstructured interview can lead to issues being uncovered that would not otherwise have come to light, purely because the conversation has flowed in a certain direction and because individuals tend to relax and talk more openly in an

Top tips for writing subject-specific needs analysis questionnaires

1. Keep it short and simple.
2. Be clear about the information that you want to gather and ensure that all your questions relate to this.
3. Use closed questions or ranking questions if you want to carry out statistical analysis on the replies.
4. Use open questions if you want to gain qualitative information.
5. Use language that the learners will understand – avoid technical jargon that may only be used by highly competent people.
6. Provide individuals with time and space to complete the questionnaires.
7. Give some incentive for completing the questionnaire and state the deadline for return.
8. Consider whether the questionnaires should be anonymous or named – this may have an impact on the honesty with which they are completed.
9. Ask questions about the current and future relevance of the subject to the potential learner and the level of skill or knowledge – this will help to prioritize the needs.

unstructured interview. Having said this, the information gained from this form of interview can take time to sift through and analyse.

Although mainly held on an individual basis, interviews can be conducted with groups, often called focus groups. The difference would be the purpose and level of the needs analysis – group interviews are particularly useful when you want to assess team or group needs. Group interviews have other benefits: they can speed up the process of data collection, and group discussion can trigger more thoughts about different needs that had not been previously considered and also show commitment to involvement and consultation.

Performance appraisal

The appraisal process is about reviewing how someone has performed against their targets, objectives and the organization's expectations. Therefore, it automatically generates information about the positive aspects of how someone has done, their key strengths, achievements and abilities, as well as their shortfalls, weaknesses and gaps in performance, which forms the basis for a conversation about why the latter exist and what needs to happen to improve the situation. This process can also provide the opportunity to review the individual's performance against the organization's competency framework. Many appraisal systems have a specific section on development needs, which form the basis of a learning plan for the individual.

Critical incident analysis

This is a process where significant events, whether negative or positive, are considered. The person or group conducting the analysis considers what happened, why it happened and the results or consequences of the event. Questions such as 'what learning came from this situation?' and 'what knowledge, skills or behaviours need to be in place in order to prevent/reproduce the situation?' are asked, thus generating information that could feed into a development plan.

Testing and retesting

For some tasks and jobs regular testing can highlight development needs. This process can be extremely time-consuming; however, it does reap rewards and does provide sound evidence that development is required. Testing is probably most appropriate in relation to skills and knowledge, ie individuals involved in operating equipment or who have to know certain legislation.

Skills matrices

This is a grid which classifies people's competency levels for each skill area required by the department or team in which they work. A simple rating system is used to indicate each person's ability in every skill area, providing a summary of who can do what and to what level. The skills matrix can then be used to identify gaps in individual ability as well as shortfalls in team skills. It is also useful for identifying people who could be used to support the development of others. An example of a skills matrix is shown in Chapter 6 as part of the 'Moneybank' case study.

Assessment and development centres

Assessment and development centres involve the participants' completing a range of activities and exercises designed to enable them to demonstrate the knowledge, skills and behaviours required in a specific role. The activities used vary from group tasks and individual exercises to psychometric tests and interviews. Assessment centres have been traditionally used for recruitment and selection, although increasingly they have a developmental element, the underpinning principle being that the most effective way of predicting how someone will perform in a future role is by getting the individual to carry out tasks that accurately reflect those required in the job. Development centres are similar to assessment centres, but their specific purpose is to assess development needs – so participants are not competing for a new role or job, but are being assessed against the competencies required for the role in order to identify areas for learning.

Assessment and development centres are good objective measures of current competency, and therefore the data gained has high validity. However, they need to be designed and managed by trained personnel, and can be expensive to run.

Error reporting and quality monitoring

Reviewing error rates and quality reports will provide information about current performance. Analysing such data will give trends and patterns that can form the basis for a focused investigation, which may lead to conclusions about skills and knowledge deficits.

Review of business plans

Organizational and departmental business plans must be reviewed to establish whether achievement of any of the targets will require learning and development to take place. This will be high-level information and can be checked or validated by using some of the methods above.

Having now identified the development needs, the next stage is to select methods through which these needs can be met. We have already said that every individual will have a different starting point, and therefore may need a different approach or method of learning and this is explored in Chapter 3. In Chapter 4 we offer you a range of different development methods from which to choose and go on in Chapter 5 to discuss the factors involved in making a choice of method(s).

3

An Introduction to Adult Learning

In order for you to be able to make decisions about the best learning and development methods to use, it will be helpful to consider how adults learn and what makes some methods more appropriate than others in different situations and for different people.

Below are summaries of some of the best-known theories relating to adult learning and the variety of learning preferences exhibited by individuals.

KNOWLEDGE, SKILLS AND ATTITUDES – BLOOM'S TAXONOMY

It is generally accepted that learning occurs in three distinct domains:

1 Cognitive (knowledge): this relates to the acquisition and application of knowledge and understanding. It deals mainly with learning of an intellectual nature, covering the range from simple recall through to analysis and evaluation of information.
2 Psychomotor (skills): this deals with the development of skills, ie anything that can be done. The levels within this domain range from competency to mastery.
3 Affective (attitudes): this is concerned with attitudes and feelings which are brought about or altered as the result of some learning experience. It deals with learning that has a substantial emotional basis and covers the range from having an awareness of feelings through to amending behaviour so that it becomes consistent with new values and beliefs.

When planning learning and development activities, objectives and outcomes are expressed in terms of the knowledge, skills or behaviours that will be demonstrated by the end of the experience; it is against these objectives that learning is measured.

KOLB'S EXPERIENTIAL LEARNING CYCLE

In order to learn from an experience, you have to go through the learning cycle. David Kolb stated that for true learning to take place, we need to have an experience, reflect upon this experience, make sense of it (often through creating theories) and finally apply our theories to our lives by planning what we would do next time we were in the same or similar situation. Sometimes you may go through this cycle unconsciously. Planned development processes involve bringing all four stages into consciousness and ensuring that the process of learning is completed. Learning is inhibited when a learner misses one of Kolb's stages.

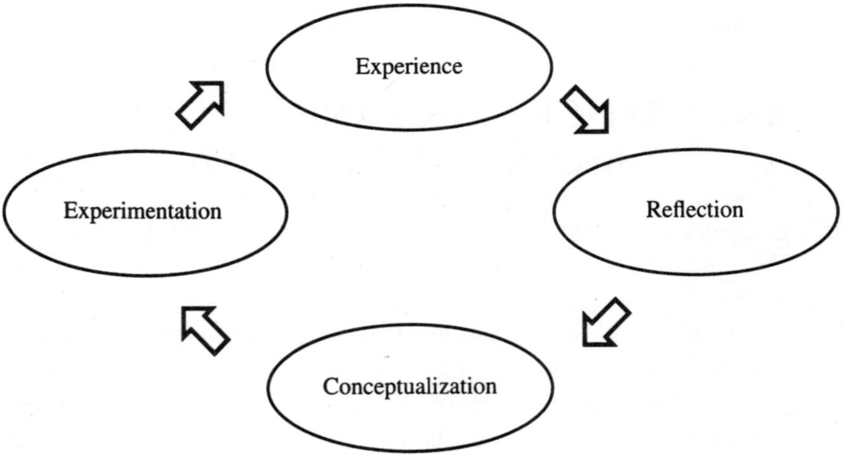

Figure 3.1 Kolb's learning cycle

HONEY AND MUMFORD'S LEARNING STYLES

Peter Honey and Alan Mumford identified four individual learning styles. Learners often demonstrate a preference for one these styles, although note the word 'preference'. Learners may adopt their secondary style, and preferred styles may change over time based upon the context and experiences of the learner. The four learning styles map onto Kolb's learning cycle.

Activists are people who learn through doing and prefer activity-based development. They dislike sitting still for long periods and will therefore not respond well to lectures or highly reflective activity. Activists are chatty, lively and like to be involved – they enjoy the 'here and now'. The methods through which they will prefer to learn involve exercises, problems, tasks, drama and excitement.

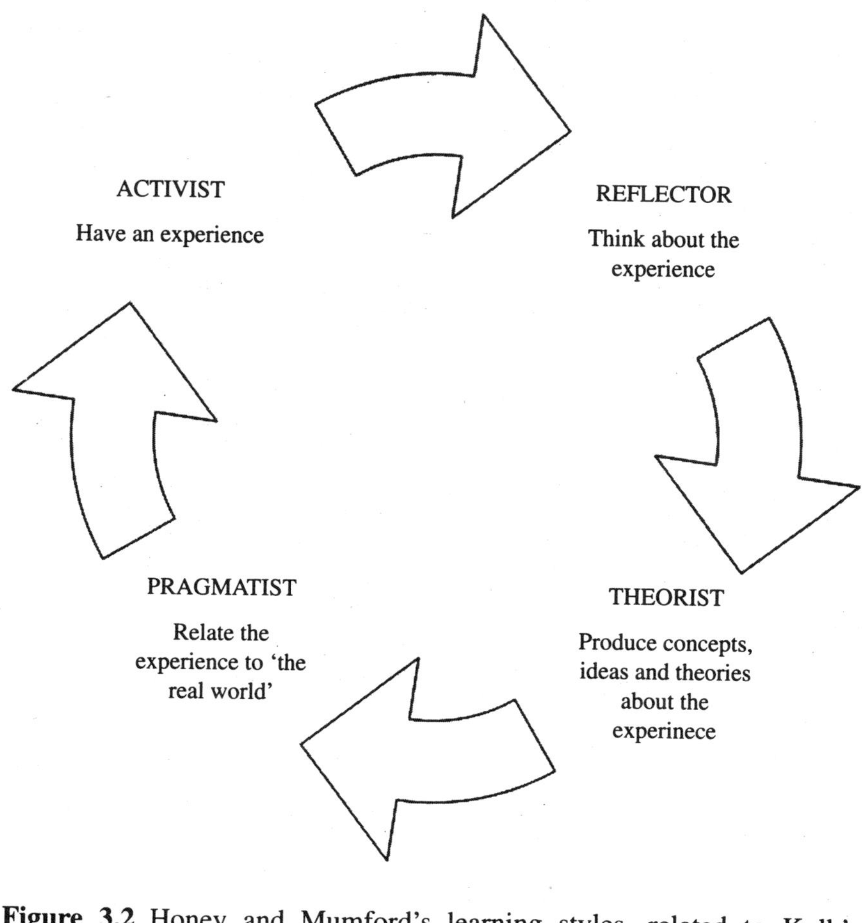

Figure 3.2 Honey and Mumford's learning styles, related to Kolb's learning cycle

Reflectors enjoy reviewing and considering situations and events. When asked a question, they tend to sit back and think about the answer before responding. In groups they will observe and reflect rather than actively join or lead the discussion. When they join a discussion their contribution will be well thought out. Reflective learners like to consider issues from a range of different perspectives and will feel uncomfortable if they are put into the limelight without prior warning; when choosing methods for them, ensure that they will have the time required for reflection to take place.

Theorists like to know the theories behind a piece of learning or the ideas that back up comments that are being made. They prefer to learn from research, data, models and information. They do not cope well when they are asked to do something without being told why and without underpinning evidence or theory. Theorists like logic and are rational and analytical – in a learning situation, they like their development activities to have structure and purpose; they will be uncomfortable with high emotion and feelings.

Pragmatists prefer practicality to theory and learn effectively when they are able to apply the learning to their situation and the real world. They learn best when provided with true-to-life tasks, rather than being given 'woolly' concepts that they are unable to relate to their daily life. They seek out new ideas and want to try them out, drawing links between the subject and their current job.

Learners with a strong preference for one or more of the learning styles are more likely to remain at the stage of learning most closely aligned with their preference. This means that they will not complete the learning cycle and consequently their learning may not be as effective as it would be if they experienced all the stages. So whilst it is important to match learning methods with preferred learning styles, a development plan should encourage the learner to practise using styles and methods that they are not necessarily comfortable with.

SENSORY LEARNING PREFERENCES

Learning takes place when we receive and process information. There are five senses through which the human body receives stimuli – taste, smell, hearing, touch and seeing; in terms of communication and learning, it is the last three that have particular relevance. Each of us has a preference about the way in which we like to communicate – these are described as:

1 Visual: this is a preference for seeing and visualizing. Learners who have a visual preference will like pictures and diagrams. They will create mental pictures in order to be able to understand what they are being told. The language that they tend to use and respond to includes visual words such as 'I see', 'What would that look like?' and 'I can't picture that'.
2 Auditory: this is a preference for hearing and words. Learners with an auditory preference will want to have concepts explained to them; presenting them with a diagram will not be sufficient. They will respond well to discussions, music and written material. In terms of language that you will hear from auditory learners, phrases such as 'I hear what you're saying', 'can you explain that to me?' and 'that sounds good' are useful clues.
3 Kinaesthetic: individuals with this preference appreciate activities and the opportunity to move about because they tend to communicate best through doing, touching and feeling. They will use terms linked to touch such as 'that grabs me!', 'I feel comfortable with that' or 'I can relate to that'.

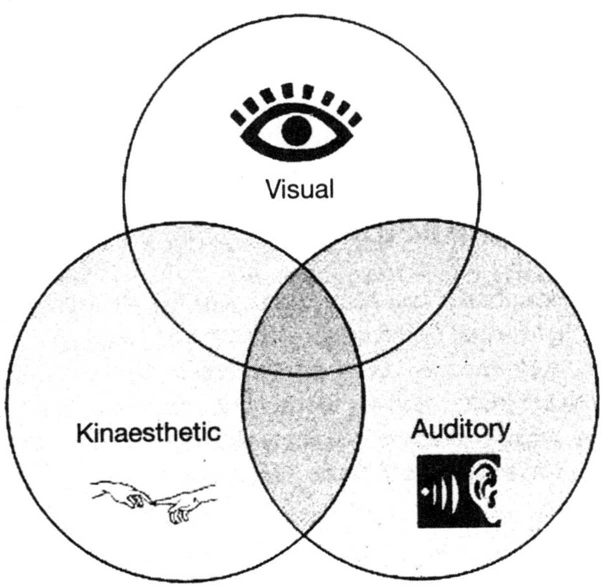

Figure 3.3 Sensory learning preferences

As with Honey and Mumford's learning styles, these are preferences and do not prevent the absorption of information via all the senses; however, being aware of a person's style gives valuable clues to the type of development methods that will work for them.

THEORY OF COMPETENCE

This theory states that learning is a four-stage process, which involves the journey from unconscious incompetence to unconscious competence.

Unconscious incompetence

This is where you are unaware that you do not know something or cannot do it – it is the 'I don't know what I don't know' level. There is probably little need or requirement for you to have the skill or knowledge in question at this time, and this is why you have not yet developed the awareness of your lack of competence.

Conscious incompetence

This is where you become aware of your lack of competence in a certain area. This is the stage of 'I know what I don't know'. This usually happens because you have a need or a desire to do something new or differently. You may become aware through your own observations, a desire to progress, an impending change, or through feedback from others.

Conscious competence

To become consciously competent you will go through some form of learning – either formal or informal. Often at this stage you will do things in exactly the way you have been shown how to do them (subject to your memory). You are aware at every moment of everything that you are doing – you 'know what you know'. Your application of the learning will be limited to the ways and situations in which you learnt it.

Unconscious competence

This is where your knowledge and skills have been used so often they are 'habits' – you don't need to think about the next part of the process as it is stored in the unconscious (or subconscious) part of your brain. It is the 'I don't know what I know' stage, and people who are very competent at a task or skill are often unable to explain what and how they do it.

The learning curve and competency

In order to select appropriate methods of development, it will help if you are aware of what stage the learner is at. See Figure 3.4, the learning curve.

As the learner moves up the learning curve, they become more competent and therefore different methods become more relevant and appropriate. For example, if you are learning to make presentations, at the consciously incompetent stage you may need a training course to learn the techniques.

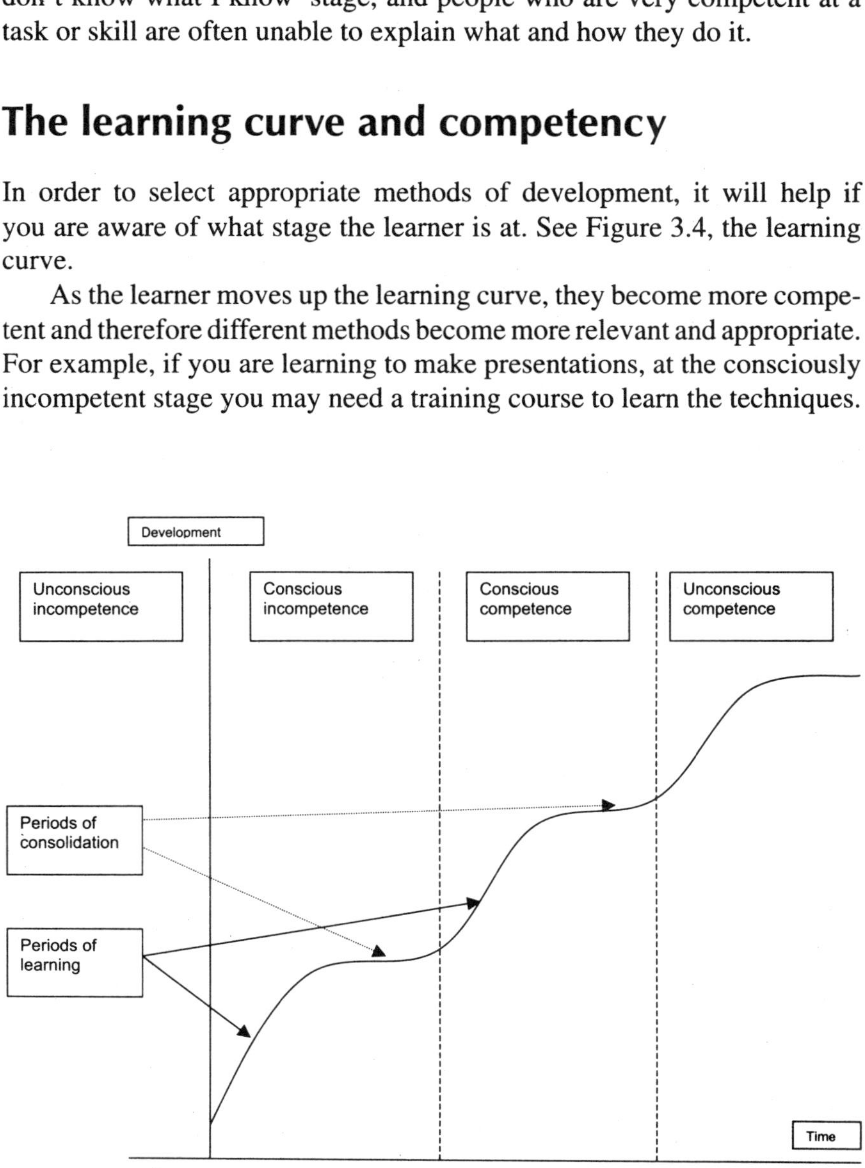

Figure 3.4 The learning curve

Once you become consciously competent, the learning can be embedded by practice and coaching. Once you become unconsciously competent, benefit can be gained via reflective practice, observation of others and/or mentoring.

The time it takes for the learner to achieve the required standard (sometimes known as the Experienced Worker Standard) depends upon:

- the effectiveness of the learning process;
- the experience of the learner – the starting point and the prior knowledge;
- the learner's natural aptitude;
- the learner's interest and motivation.

MOTIVATING ADULTS TO LEARN

Research carried out by Fiona Aldridge for the National Institute of Adult Continuing Education (NIACE) identified three broad categories of learning, each with their own motivators:

Table 3.1

Category of learning	Potential motivators
Work related	Gain more money Enhance promotion prospects Achieve greater job satisfaction
Personal development	Achieve self-improvement Learn for pleasure Increase self-confidence
Education	Gain a qualification Access further education

In order to learn effectively, adults must want to learn, understand the purpose of the learning and be engaged with the process. The stimulus creating the desire to learn can be negative or positive – it can be a threat, an unacceptable consequence or a perceived reward, such as moving up the pay scale, achieving a promotion or gaining recognition by others or self. Hopefully it goes without saying that if the stimulus is positive, learning will be more enjoyable.

ORGANIZATIONAL LEARNING

Organizations that do not learn faster than the rate of change in the environment will eventually die.

Reg Revans

There are many definitions of organizational learning. We see it as learning, however it happens, that influences how the organization works. Organizational learning may change culture, processes, procedures, systems and/or practices; as such, it impacts upon the performance of the whole organization.

Organizational learning can take place at two levels: single loop learning is about dealing with the problems or symptoms of a situation, rather than the underlying cause. This is about doing things right. Double loop learning examines the underlying causes of a situation, which may lead to a review of the organization's assumptions and goals. This is about doing the right things.

So what does this mean in terms of this book – a book about different development methods and the transition from training to learning? We have already discussed how encouraging individuals to develop has an impact on the growth and sustainability of an organization. To be of value to an organization development has to provide return on investment – you must maximize the potential for learning to take place. This involves creating the right climate for learning and development to occur and includes understanding how adults receive, absorb and make sense of information, experiences and situations. For growth to occur, you need to have the right growing medium!

In order to achieve effective organizational learning, individual learning is not enough. Learning that takes place at an individual level must be brought into the context of the team and the wider organization so that it can influence practices and change within that organization, ie the organization does something that it could not do before or knows something that it didn't know before. This ability to consciously adapt and respond is effective organizational learning. When creating a learning and development strategy, consideration should be given to the ways in which individual learning will be shared and used across the organization.

4

Learning and Development Methods

This chapter details various methods by which groups and individuals can learn. Each method is described as follows:

- What the method involves
- Use it because...
- Making it work
- It is useful for...

Where applicable we have also included a list of references and/or further reading.

ACTION LEARNING

Professor Reginald W. Revans came up with the concept of action learning whilst working as a research physicist and then applied it to industry whilst working for the National Coal Board in the UK in the late 1940s/early 1950s. The basis of action learning is an equation:

$$L = P + Q$$

Where
L = learning;
P = programmed knowledge – the knowledge that already exists and can be gained by reading books or using other research methods to access theories and concepts;
Q = questioning insight – the application of questions about a situation and how the programmed knowledge might apply to that situation.

In other words, action learning is based on the premise that learning will take place when existing knowledge is applied to a problem through the use of questioning.

Action learning is more than learning by doing; this is because it involves all aspects of the learning cycle, including reflection about what has been learnt, internalization of the learning and its pragmatic application to the situation at hand. Because the learning has been assimilated and processed, it is more likely that it can be applied to new and different situations.

Action learning will only work effectively when it is applied to a problem that does not yet have a solution. It is useful for situations which are complex and where there is no one willing to step forward to offer a way out. Because action learning is a time-consuming and rather complex process in itself, it will only work when participants and their managers are committed to it.

Action learning takes place in so-called action learning sets. These sets are small groups of people (usually about six people) brought together for the specific purpose of learning through solving a problem – rather than solving a problem with learning as an added bonus. Action learning will appeal to all learning styles because it involves activity, application of theory to practical situations and reflection, both on theory and on reality.

The following is an example of a process that could be used to implement action learning:

1 *Define the problem.* This step will be taken by the 'problem-owner' – this is the person who will bring the problem to the action learning set. The problem owner asks themself – 'What tells us that there is a problem? What are the results that we would like to see in this situation and what is stopping these results from being achieved?'
2 *Set up the action learning set.* Bring together a diverse group of individuals who have a mixture of skills and backgrounds. Appoint a facilitator, whose role it will be to keep the group focused on the problem and encourage reflection so that learning takes place.
3 *Present the problem.* The 'problem-owner' will outline the problem to the action learning set and then becomes a member of the learning set.
4 *Ask questions.* Learning set members analyse the problem and its causes using a series of open, probing, clarifying questions. Questioning will then be used to redefine the problem and the required outcome.
5 *Prepare action plans.* Learning set members work together offering theories, concepts and ideas in ways which are applied to the problem and the required outcome. The group then produces a list of actions that can be applied to the problem.

6 *Implement the action plan.* During the implementation of the action plan, the learning set meets on a regular basis in order to reflect upon what is working, what is not working and how effective the overall plan is being in resolving the problem. The action plan can be amended as a result of these reflections.
7 *Review and reflect.* Reflection on what has been learnt is a key part of the action learning process and takes place at all meetings of the learning set. This is what makes the process different from problem solving. Supporting this reflective practice is one of the key roles of the learning set facilitator.

Use it because...

- It provides an opportunity for individuals from a variety of areas to work together creatively and promotes team and individual development.
- It can provide timely solutions to complex and difficult current problems which are impacting upon organizations and teams.
- Action learning supports the development of a learning organization by demonstrating that learning takes place whilst dealing with real-life issues.
- Working on a real problem provides measurable outputs and a demonstrable return on investment.
- By promoting cross-functional and multi-level working, it encourages responsibility for learning and problem solving without relying on hierarchy.

Making it work

Action learning sets work most effectively when:

- Processes and parameters that will be followed are laid down at the start of the programme.
- Sufficient time is set aside for the process to take place and participants are released from their workplace to attend. This requires total commitment from both participants and their line managers.
- Participants volunteer to be part of the programme and they have faith that the action learning process can really work and that it is not simply 'another training exercise'.
- A facilitator is appointed to each learning set. This should be someone who has some experience and skill in the area of facilitation and who is

sufficiently capable of keeping the learning set on track, whilst promoting creativity and reflection without allowing 'analysis-paralysis' or 'navel-gazing' to set in.
- The facilitator does not allow one or two individuals to dominate the group.
- The learning set is focused on real, not theoretical, problems or issues.
- The learning set has the time and opportunity to go through some kind of group-building process.
- The learning set has a specific objective which is clearly defined.
- The learning set is made up of individuals who feel able to work together at the same level, despite their position within the organizational structure.
- No learning set member feels that he or she has the answer to the problem under consideration.
- The organization is willing for the learning set to put in place their action plan in order for their ideas to be tested, revised and retested.

It is useful for...

- Organizations that wish to instil a flexible and creative approach to learning and problem solving.
- Individuals with activist and pragmatist learning styles who will appreciate the focus on real-life scenarios and the opportunity to implement an action plan.
- Learners who have reflective and theorist learning styles, because they will have the opportunity to think about issues and consider a range of theories and ideas.
- Organizations that comprise a high number of specialist roles.

References and further reading

Brockbank, A and McGill, I (2003) *The Action Learning Handbook: Powerful techniques for education, professional development and training*, Routledge Falmer, London

McGill, I and Beaty, L (2000) *Action Learning: A practitioner's guide*, Routledge Falmer, London

Pedler, M (1996) *Action Learning for Managers*, Lemos and Crane, London

Revans, R W (1980) *Action Learning*, Frederick Muller Ltd, London
Rothwell, W J (1999) *Action Learning Guidebook*, Jossey-Bass/Pfeiffer, San Francisco
Weinstein, K (1998) *Action Learning: A practical guide*, Gower, Aldershot

APPRENTICESHIPS

Apprenticeships have existed since the Middle Ages when the first guilds of craftsmen were established. Today, apprenticeships take on two forms – those that involve government funding and support, and those that are set up by organizations as part of their ongoing development programmes. The aim of an apprenticeship is to build the skills that an employer needs in order to sustain the productivity of the organization and to develop for the future.

An apprenticeship has three distinctive elements:

1 It involves on-the-job training.
2 The apprentice has the opportunity to earn whilst they are learning.
3 Its focus is on the employer and the needs of the employing organization.

Government-funded apprenticeships

In the UK, apprenticeships were relaunched by the government in May 2004 as a key part of their strategy to develop the skills that had been identified for future success. The document 'Blueprint for Apprenticeships', published in September 2005, identifies that there are three key stakeholders in the apprenticeship – the employer, the apprentice and the government. The role of the employer is to provide the workplace for the apprentice, to support their learning and provide their wages. The apprentice commits to participating in training and accepts a lower wage during the training period. The government funds the learning that the apprentice receives. Learning is provided by designated 'learning providers' who will work in partnership with the three key stakeholders to ensure that learning activities meet the needs and are of the required standard. The document also identifies the requirements of any government-funded apprenticeship which are:

- a competence-based element;
- a knowledge-based element;

- transferable ('key') skills;
- employment rights and responsibilities.

Government-funded apprenticeships were initially available for individuals aged between 16 and 24. Discussions are ongoing about funding for adult apprenticeships for those aged 25 and over.

Organization-funded apprenticeships

An apprenticeship can be set up by any employer who wishes to offer long-term development programmes. Before embarking on such a scheme, organizations should consider the following questions:

1 What are the required outcomes for the scheme?
2 What other methods would be available to achieve the same outcomes?
3 How much will it cost to implement the scheme (recruitment costs, training costs, wage costs, internal resource requirements, oncosts etc)?
4 Who will manage the scheme?
5 How will the apprentices be recruited and monitored?
6 How will the apprentices be trained?
7 What return on investment is required and within what time period?
8 What are the risks involved in implementing the scheme and how can these risks be managed?
9 What changes might occur that will impact upon the scheme?

Use it because...

Some of the benefits for organizations in becoming involved in apprenticeship schemes are outlined by the Learning and Skills Council on their website. They include:

- Improved productivity – because apprentices are equipped with knowledge and practical skills, they will be more productive for their employers because they will be able to perform more effectively and efficiently. Because the individuals are likely to be more motivated, they will work harder and with more commitment.
- Relevant training – apprenticeship schemes are designed to provide training that is relevant to the needs of the employers and will support the need to recruit and retain skilled staff.

- Avoid skills shortages – apprenticeships will allow employers to fill skills gaps and avoid future skills shortages because they are focused on building skills for the future.

The apprentice benefits because:

- they are able to gain new skills and qualifications whilst working;
- they have the opportunity to gain real work experience which will enhance their career development possibilities and consolidate their learning;
- they can find out what it is like to work for a particular organization or within a particular field.

Making it work

- Fully plan the content of the apprenticeship, including requirements in terms of the finance, time and resources needed to set up, administer and monitor the scheme. If applicable, research and secure government funding.
- Allocate time out for off-job training and education.
- Appoint a coordinator who will be responsible for the paperwork and administration associated with government-funded training or alternatively monitoring in-house apprentices.
- At the start of the programme, agree what will happen to the apprentices at the end of the scheme in order to manage the expectations of all stakeholders. Consider whether there will be permanent jobs and where these will be located.

It is useful for...

- Organizations that have entry-level positions available for school-leavers.
- Future manpower planning where there is no need for fully qualified people at present, but the strategic plans indicate that a need will exist in the mid-term future.
- Bringing in 'new blood' and to undertake some long-term succession planning.

Reference and further reading

Learning and Skills Council, www.lsc.gov.uk

COACHING

Coaching has grown in popularity in recent years. In the CIPD annual learning and development survey report of 2006, 79 per cent of organizations that responded stated that they now use coaching. The survey goes on to identify that of the organizations using coaching, 80 per cent say that they aspire to develop a coaching culture and 47 per cent indicated that they are training line managers to act as coaches.

Coaching is a technique in its own right and should not be confused with on-job training, mentoring or counselling. There are probably as many 'varieties' of coaching as there are coaches; however, for the context of this book, we are referring to work-based coaching as opposed to life coaching or sports coaching, to name two examples.

In our previous book *The Coaching Handbook* (Kogan Page 2003), we defined coaching as 'the process of helping people enhance or improve their performance through reflection on how they apply a specific skill and/or knowledge'.

Coaching is a 1:1 activity and can take place on the job or away from the workplace. It is about applying the skills and knowledge already learnt to a specific situation, thus resulting in an improvement in performance. There are many models and techniques used in coaching; essentially coaching is about a relationship between the coach and coachee which provides opportunities for the coachee to reflect upon what they have experienced in order to learn from that experience and develop their capabilities.

True coaching is something that is systematically planned and carried out. It takes place over a fixed period of time and has a distinct beginning, middle and end. The process of coaching, whichever model is selected, will include the following stages:

Stage 1: Clarifying the need
Stage 2: Agreeing specific development objectives
Stage 3: Formulating a detailed plan
Stage 4: Doing a task or activity
Stage 5: Reviewing and planning improvements
Repetition of stages 3, 4, and 5 as required
Stage 6: Ending the coaching relationship.

Use it because...

- Coaching is targeted to meet individual needs and is therefore more likely to produce immediate results.
- It enables the coachee to apply their skills, knowledge and behaviours to a real-life situation, thereby increasing their effectiveness as they can either apply new learning to their present situation or use existing skills in a different way.
- Coaching can be carried out at times and in locations that suit the coachee, their manager and their organization.
- Line managers can act as coaches for their staff and for other staff within their organization. This develops the line managers and makes the process cost-effective for the organization.
- Peer coaching is a good way of enhancing performance whilst promoting mutual learning and development.
- Coaching can be used to address rapidly changing situations within organizations and can therefore help support any major changes that are taking place.
- Coaching can support individuals who are making decisions or dealing with conflict situations – it can provide a forum to try out new ideas in a safe and supportive environment.
- It provides individuals with the opportunity to reflect upon their current performance and identify areas for development.
- The nature of the coaching relationship will make the coachee feel valued, supported and encouraged that their employer is placing real emphasis on their individual development.

Making it work

- Ensure that coaching is the appropriate development method by carrying out an assessment of the learner's current skills – if the coachee does not have the basic skills and knowledge before the coaching begins, the coach may find themselves slipping into training mode, which they may not be prepared for. Coaching is likely to be the preferred option when you are able to answer 'yes' to the following questions:
  - Does the person already have the skills and knowledge to perform this task?
  - Will the person be performing the task/using the skills or knowledge in the near future?
  - If this person undertakes work on a one-to-one basis, will it help them enhance or improve their performance?

- Define what is meant by the term coaching – coaching is often confused with mentoring, counselling and/or line management, therefore the expectations and perceptions of the process will be wrong from the start.
- Select the right coach for the individual learner to ensure that the relationship develops effectively. Rapport is important to ensuring honesty, two-way communication and effective feedback. Consider whether it is more appropriate to use an external coach.
- Deliver the coaching in a timely manner, ie just before the person will be required to carry out the task or use the skill that the coaching focuses on.
- Set ground rules for the coaching relationship and define the process that will take place. Create a coaching contract that includes roles and responsibilities for the coach and coachee as well as detailing the communication that will take place with third parties such as the coachee's line manager, HR departments and colleagues. The coaching contract should also include agreed learning objectives and expected performance outcomes as well as the evaluation method to be used.
- Allocate time for the coach and coachee to prepare as well as time for the coaching sessions.
- Make a space available for the coaching sessions that is comfortable and offers privacy.

It is useful for...

- *Enhancing performance.* Coaching is about helping individuals to improve their performance by developing the ways in which they use their knowledge and skills. This may be needed because they are not applying them to the required standard or because they are required to use them in a new context.
- *Transferring learning.* When an individual has attended a training course to acquire new skills or knowledge, coaching is useful to support them as they apply and consolidate their learning.
- *Inducting new employees.* Coaching can be used to help someone to settle into a new role, whether recruited internally or externally.
- *Managing talent.* Individuals who have been identified as 'high-flyers' or tomorrow's leaders can benefit from coaching in order to prepare them for their future careers.
- *Supporting senior managers.* Executive coaching is used with senior managers because many of their development needs are very specific and unique to the individuals and to the organization. We discuss executive coaching as a separate development method.

- *Developing 'soft' skills.* Coaching is particularly effective when dealing with 'soft' skills because there is no hard and fast way of doing things and coaching provides the opportunity to discuss behaviour and impact in a supportive and non-judgemental arena.

References and further reading

Caplan, J (2003) *Coaching for the Future: How smart companies use coaching and mentoring,* CIPD, London

CIPD Annual Survey Report 2006 Learning and Development: www.cipd.co.uk/surveys

Clutterbuck, D and Megginson, D (2005) How to create a coaching culture, *People Management,* **11** (8), 21 April, pp 44–45

Cunningham, I and Dawes, G (1999) *Assessing your Coaching Capability,* Topics for Trainers, CIPD, London. Available at: http://www.cipd.co.uk/subjects/lrnanddev/coachmntor/asscoach.htm

Davidson, S (2002) How to... choose the right coach, *People Management,* **8** (10), 16 May, pp 54–55

Hardingham, A, Brearley, M and Moorhouse, A (2004) *The Coach's Coach: Personal development for personal developers,* CIPD, London

Jarvis, J (2004) *Coaching and Buying Coaching Services. A guide*, CIPD, London. Available at: http://www.cipd.co.uk/guides

Kubicek, M (2004) Be one step ahead. *Training Magazine*, October, pp 21–23

Lee, G (2004) How to buy coaching. *People Management*, **10** (5), 11 March, pp 50–51

Thorpe, S and Clifford, J (2003) *The Coaching Handbook: An action kit for trainers and managers,* Kogan Page, London

DELEGATION

Delegation is the process by which a line manager empowers an individual to perform certain duties. This can be a very powerful development tool, as the individual is carrying out the task or skill that they are trying to learn – it is giving someone real work in a real situation which means they can properly learn how to do it and consequently gain confidence and competency.

Unfortunately, delegation is one of those terms that has been much overused and consequently wrongly used. Delegation is not the same as allocating tasks and work. It does not mean offloading work and leaving people to get on with it with no support. Successful delegation is about supporting the individual so that they are able to carry out a task or job that would normally be yours – it involves giving them support, training if needed, authority and responsibility, whilst you retain the accountability for ensuring it is done properly and on time.

There are four stages to effective delegation:

Stage 1: Planning:

- What is the task?
- Who are you going to delegate to? Why? What is the benefit to them?
- What do they need to know – about the delegation process and the task itself?
- What are the details of the task? Deadlines? Procedures? Statutory or company requirements? Where does it fit the bigger process? What flexibility exists around how the task is carried out?
- When will you meet with them to brief them and review progress?
- What are your expectations? What are the required outcomes?

Stage 2: Briefing the learner

- Explain what you plan to do and why you have chosen them.
- Agree outcomes and set guidelines.
- Explain the task and if possible demonstrate where appropriate.
- Allow freedom. Let go sufficiently so that the learner can use their initiative – they do not have to be you.
- Allow them to question and explore.
- Check understanding. Make sure that you both understand what the other means.
- Have realistic expectations. They are learning so it is unlikely to be perfect!
- Agree progress reports, review meetings and contact time.
- Discuss difficult areas. If in doubt, check out understanding. Do not assume that just because they say they understand, they do.

Stage 3: Monitor progress

- Do not interfere. Stand back and monitor. Be available if required.
- Encourage them to do things their own way and to explore.
- Be alert for things going wrong. Monitor the situation – be ready to step in to support and advise.
- Tolerate trivial mistakes.
- Be available to help and advise, but only when you are asked or absolutely must because the situation has become critical. Don't just step in, as that is simply annoying!

- Encourage frequent informal discussions.
- Stand back; observe what is happening from a distance. Try to get an overall picture of what is happening as if you are hovering above the action in a helicopter.

Stage 4: Evaluation and feedback
- Give praise.
- Give feedback. Make sure the feedback is constructive and refers to a specific behaviour or action. Do not attack the person or criticize them solely for doing things differently from how you would do them when it doesn't matter.
- Help everyone learn from the experience.
- Accept accountability. Remember you delegate the authority and the responsibility but not the accountability.

Use it because…

- Delegation develops individual skills and knowledge – it enables a person to learn new skills and use their existing ones on different tasks.
- Delegation can make time available for the manager to develop and take on new tasks.
- It encourages a learning culture by embedding development into everyday activity, with responsibility for learning resting with the managers and their staff. It empowers individuals and teams to engage with the process of continuous development, and not wait for someone 'to do it to them'.
- It can promote team development by having more people able to carry out more of the tasks, and therefore absence or turnover will have less impact. It also improves communication between the manager and their staff, because successful delegation is based on effective communication.
- Getting different people to carry out tasks can lead to creativity and better ways of doing things – inbuilt into the process of delegation is review – why is it done this way? This means that processes can be improved and new ideas generated.
- Organizations can identify strengths and weaknesses within their staff resources, which can help with succession planning.
- The individual gets to apply their learning straightaway and get immediate feedback on whether they have done it correctly, and how they can improve next time, within the safety of a development context.

Making it work

- *Do it despite the fear.* Many managers dislike delegating. The reasons are well documented but can be summarized as 'fear' – fear of losing control, fear of not having enough to do, fear of someone else doing it better! However, the benefits of delegation far outweigh the potential pitfalls. Following the systematic process will enable you to reduce the possibility of failing and this in turn should reduce some of your anxiety.
- *Communicate effectively with the learner.* Successful delegation is reliant upon a good working relationship. Consider how they need to receive information so that you can explain what needs doing in the most appropriate way for them. Agree with them how you will check progress, when you will give feedback, and use open questions to check understanding.
- *Use delegation as a development tool not a dumping ground.* Sometimes delegation is used to offload work or set someone up with an impossible situation, rather than to help them develop. Check your motivations before you delegate a task, and be clear at all times about the purpose.
- *Allocate sufficient time.* Time is required, both from the delegating manager and the learner. Allocate time to explain the task as well as time to carry it out, bearing in mind that the first few times the work is done, it will be done more slowly than you would normally do it. It is also important that a review of the learner's total workload is carried out so that they are not overloaded and you are just adding another piece of work to an already full job. It may be necessary for you to give one of their jobs to someone else before you start delegating – this might involve them learning to delegate to another person, before they can be delegated to.
- *Be aware of your timing.* Consider where the individual is in their development and what else is happening for them at this time to ensure that they are ready to learn in this way.
- *Check the starting point.* Does the learner have the underpinning knowledge and skills required to carry out this new work? If not, when and how will they gain these?

It is useful for...

- Developing someone who has been assessed as ready to take on a more complex or senior role, and learning this task will assist with their transition.

- Motivating a member of staff who needs a new challenge, different work to do or is getting bored.
- Activists and pragmatists, who enjoy this method of experiential learning.
- Assessing whether someone is ready for more responsibility or promotion.

References and further reading

Armstrong, M (2004) *How to be an Even Better Manager: A complete A-Z of proven techniques and essential skills*, 6th edn, Kogan Page, London

Brown, C L (1997) *Essential Delegation Skills* (The Smart Management Guides series), Gower Publishing Ltd, London

Keenan, K (1996) *The Management Guide to Delegating*, Ravette Publishing, Horsham

Smart, J K (2002) *Real Delegation: How to get people to do things for you – and to do them well*, Prentice Hall, London

DISCUSSION BOARDS AND GROUPS

These groups bring together members who have a common interest in talking about a specific subject, in order to share their experience, exchange ideas, solve problems and/or gain support.

Traditionally, discussion groups would have a formal or informal meeting format, and alternative names are: lunch and share, breakfast forums, conferences, work-groups. In our technological age, discussion forums are now internet based and are called discussion boards, chat rooms, noticeboards or virtual learning environments. Many universities, professional bodies and distance learning organizations are using virtual learning environments to support their students (for example, the Open University and Ashridge).

Use it because...

Discussion groups are an opportunity to share knowledge and experiences; with technology this can be gained from a wider audience without the expense of travelling, or the limitation of knowing whom to invite. They can offer a place to ask for help or to check understanding, which may not be available within an organization. Individuals can build a support network with others who have their specialism or expertise. There is no formal hierarchy in discussion groups (if created well) and this means that each member can contribute as they feel able, rather than worry about being judged by senior members of their organizations.

Making it work

- Establish ground rules, guidelines and etiquette for your group.
- If you are setting up an internet discussion board, appoint a moderator, who can review postings and ensure that they are relevant and consistent with legal requirements and the guidelines of your site. The moderator can also act as a facilitator to encourage input from all members rather than allowing a clique to form and take action to clarify misunderstandings that can arise from communicating via the written word.
- In a face-to-face discussion group, use a facilitator, or chair, to keep the group on the subject, encourage wide involvement and discourage domination or sabotage.
- In any discussion there are ups and downs in the momentum and interest – don't be too worried if this happens, as it is natural and reflects the needs of the group at the time.
- Make the groups as accessible as possible in a way that suits your organization. Be aware of access to the internet or intranet, and also consider the working times of staff for discussion group meetings. Internet discussions work well for staff who are out and about or work shifts so long as they have access to the relevant technology. Some organizations prefer early morning meetings, others like lunchtime sessions. Staff requirements in different departments may vary; for example, taking people out first thing in the morning may work for a finance department but not a call centre.

It is useful for...

- Bringing people from different locations together so they can share their ideas and experiences. This can be done virtually or in person depending upon their location, your resources and the overall purpose.
- Increasing specialist knowledge or skills, by giving access to others in a specific function or specialist area.

- Situations where there is a problem to be solved – this may be a technical problem that requires specialists to sit and consider it, or a more general issue that requires people with different expertise to have input.

DISTANCE LEARNING

We are using the term 'distance learning' to cover formal structured courses that are studied away from an academic institution. The Open and Distance Learning Quality Council gives the following definition on their website:

> *Open and distance learning includes any provision in which a significant element of the management of the provision is at the discretion of the learner, supported and facilitated by the provider. This ranges from traditional correspondence courses, on-line provision and interactive CD ROMs, e-learning and blended learning to open learning centres and face-to-face provision where a significant element of flexibility, self-study, and learning support, is an integral part.*

Distance learning is closely related to self-study and e-learning in that it is a process where learners are provided with a package of materials and often tutor support which they work through at their own pace and in their own environment. It is usually structured with a variety of formative (ongoing) and summative (at the end of units or modules) assessments. The Open University is the best known of the distance learning providers (over the past 10 years other learning providers have increased their use of this method) and their courses increasingly make use of internet-based methods such as discussion groups, access to online materials and tutorial support. The government-funded project Learndirect makes extensive use of distance learning packages, many of which are delivered through e-learning (see e-learning section).

Distance learning packages can lead to the award of an academic qualification and provide access to such qualifications for those unable to participate in full- or part-time education. There are other distance learning packages that do not lead to a qualification. Although many of these are very good, it needs to be noted that the quality assurance of these packages may not be monitored by an external body.

Companies often like to support this method of learning as it enables the employee to attend work every day and does not interfere with staffing levels.

Use it because...

- Distance learning provides learners with the chance to maintain a flexible schedule. Because learners are able to design their own learning schedule, they have the opportunity to learn at times and in places conducive for their particular learning preferences and lifestyles.
- Not only can learners develop their knowledge of the course content, but the course will enable them to develop learning skills as they have to take responsibility for doing the work and this method may offer the chance for the individual to use different learning technologies.
- With the introduction of online elements of distance learning, there is an opportunity to build a virtual network of others studying the same course, enabling the learner to gain the benefit of group learning without having to attend a college or off-site training course.
- Distance learning courses give the opportunity to learn from home or from work and to learn in previously 'dead' times such as the daily commute.

Making it work

- Ensure that the learner has fully thought out what they want to study and the implications of studying via distance learning. See below for a checklist that they can use to prepare for studying.
- Before the learner starts the course, ensure that the relevancy of the course has been fully explored and agreed upon. As with academic courses, the content of a distance learning programme will be prescribed and therefore its relevance to your organization may need some discussion.
- Have regular contact with the learner because it can be hard to keep motivated when trying to maintain a balance between work and personal life, and you will be able to identify and deal with any issues early if you have this contact. It is very easy to set individuals off on a course of distance learning and then to assume that they are working through the package. If there is to be any measure of return on investment it is important to monitor individual progress and to ensure that assignments and exams are completed on time.
- The learner may need more ongoing support and encouragement than someone attending an off-site course as feedback on assignments and assessments may take more time to be delivered.

Preparing for Distance Learning Checklist

1 Clarify your learning objectives and what you want to achieve by studying.
2 Ask yourself the following questions in order to consider if distance learning is right for you:
   - Do I prefer working by myself or with others?
   - How important is a classroom/training room atmosphere to my learning abilities?
   - How will I motivate myself to fulfil my educational goals?
   - What skills do I have to help me complete work that arrives in print, over the telephone, or via computer?
   - How self-motivated am I? Is this sufficient to keep me going when I am finding the course difficult or challenging, or when home life or work pressures need to take priority?
3 Carry out research into the available distance learning courses and select a course that meets your defined objectives.
4 Make a decision about how important it will be to achieve a recognized accreditation, eg through the Open University or the Open College Network.
5 If you choose an Open University course, be aware that courses begin at certain times of the year and that the modules for which you wish to enrol may not be available when you want them.
6 Consider the budget that you have available and the timescales within which you need to achieve the qualification or complete the course. Financial support may be available from your employer or you may be able to apply for a career development loan.
7 Think about the implications for you and your family/friends/hobbies if you decide to pursue a distance learning course.
8 Once the materials arrive, make a realistic study plan and ensure that you stick to it as rigidly as possible.
9 Set aside a space where you can be comfortable and which will inspire you to learn. Gather equipment that will be useful to you, eg stationery items, computer, reference books.
10 Learn to take notes that will be effective for you. Consider techniques such as mind mapping.
11 Where the course offers tutorial support, peer group support or other learning support, build this into your study plan to ensure that you take advantage of all opportunities available to you.
12 Identify support within your organization – someone who has skills, knowledge or expertise to help you with the course subject or who has studied via this method themself.
13 Ensure that you are aware of the assessment requirements of the course and ask any questions that you have sooner rather than later. Ensure that you complete assignments by the set deadline and if you are not able to do this contact the provider as soon as you are aware of any difficulties that you have – this is especially important if the course leads to a qualification.

It is useful for...

- People who cannot be released from the workplace, for all or part of the course, because of staffing levels, shift rotas or their specialist knowledge.
- Individuals who wish to study something which is not provided via the local colleges and academic institutions.
- Theorists, who will enjoy researching and reading material relating to their topic of study.
- Encouraging a learning culture, where you want to offer a wide range of learning opportunities, not all of which are directly related to the work learners carry out, and you want to minimize the impact on the workplace.

References and further reading

British Learning Association website: www.british-learning.org.uk
Open and Distance Learning Quality Council website: www.odlqc.org.uk
The Open University website: www.open.ac.uk

DRAMA-BASED LEARNING

Drama-based learning is a method of exploring skills and behaviours in an interactive, entertaining and practical way. Drama can be used to support learning in a variety of ways.

Watching professional actors play out a scene or an event

The use of professional actors offers a benefit rarely obtained by getting the learners to role-play. Actors, as a result of their own training, are able to rework the same situation in several different ways under the direction of the audience so that learners can see for themselves the potential consequences of a course of action or change of approach. Its power as a development tool comes from the opportunity to become an objective observer. The facilitator of the learning experience is able to provide the actors with direction and background about the organization and context and therefore to structure what the actors are doing; this means that there is greater likelihood that the scene will be true to your situation. Learning will take place by the participants reflecting on what they have seen and visualizing it taking place within their own situation. Once they return to the workplace, their ability to apply what they have seen demonstrated will be enhanced. This type of activity is a form of rehearsal which is as true to life as it could possibly be without the risks of trial and error in the real world.

Watching actors on a video

Using pre-recorded video, especially professionally produced films, also involves watching actors playing out a scene, but without the interaction with the audience. This means that there is no opportunity to rehearse different ways of handling situations, other than those that have been chosen by the video producers. The learning points which are focused on have been decided by the producer and not the group or facilitator. The advantage of using pre-recorded videos is that they can be used many times with groups and for individual study.

When using a video it is important for the facilitator/trainer to watch the parts of the film that they are going to use in some depth to ensure that it will meet the learning needs of the group, and it is relevant to the objectives of the event.

Role play

When used effectively and appropriately, role play is a very powerful technique because it involves the learners taking part in a situation and practising their newly learnt skills, behaviours and strategies. However, role play has been overused, and in some cases misused, to the extent that when mentioning role play to a group of learners you are quite likely to get a negative reaction.

The opportunity to practise the skills being learnt, especially soft skills such as negotiation and assertiveness, is an important part of the learning process. Introducing the group to a 'practice session' can take some of the fear and discomfort away for individual participants. A practice session involves being yourself, identifying a situation where you would like to practise your skills and asking someone else to take on the role of the other individuals in the situation to allow you to practise.

When introducing practice sessions into a learning event it is possible that some participants will be unable to come up with their own situation for practice and therefore it is useful to have some pre-prepared scenarios, relevant to the individuals within the group, which can be provided if needed.

Use it because...

- Drama engages with both sides of the brain, the left side which is the logical/academic side and the right side which is the creative side. By engaging with both sides of the brain in this way, learning is more likely to be remembered and therefore used.
- It enables the learners to practise real-life situations, or observe others practising, enabling them to visualize and reflect upon the consequences of different behaviours in the same situation, providing the opportunity to reflect on thoughts, feelings and reactions. This reinforces learning points and enables the learner to achieve competency more rapidly.
- Participating in actor- or learner-led role plays provides a real-life challenge within a safe environment, enabling participants to see a situation or event from someone else's point of view.
- It enables participants to learn from others in a collaborative manner.

Making it work

Using drama to support learning can be risky, especially for personal development topics, because participants can become quite emotional, especially when they are taking part fully in the activity. Therefore it is important to consider how this will be managed. The following tips will help to minimize the risk:

- Only use drama techniques when they are appropriate for the subject matter, the learning objectives and the time available.
- Only use activities and techniques that you feel comfortable with and have experienced yourself.
- Use these techniques once a good relationship has been established between the facilitator and the group and between group members.
- Consider what you will do if a highly emotional situation arises and build some contingencies into the programme. If there is a high risk of someone reacting, have a second facilitator available who can have a 1:1 with that person.
- Set ground rules for the use of drama techniques, challenge individuals to get involved, but if they are not ready for the challenge, allow them to act as observers.

- If using professional actors, be sure to provide a thorough brief and find out how they work with groups, how they take and give feedback and how they will deal with any unexpected situations.
- Consider using professional actors when learners are unlikely willingly to participate fully in role play or are likely to shy away from staying in role at the difficult moments. Although using professional actors can be costly, as can the purchase of professionally produced videos, the impact of watching can be so powerful and accelerate learning to such an extent that the cost–benefit analysis will show high returns, increasing the return on investment.
- Introduce the activity fully to the learners by explaining its purpose, how it will work and the expected outcomes, so that they can see the relevance of the activities to the overall learning event. Time must be devoted to preparing learners to take part, doing the activity and then reviewing the learning after the activity. This means that the activities can take up a big chunk of a learning programme and you must be prepared for this.

It is useful for…

- All aspects of interpersonal skills development.
- When you want individuals to see the impact that their behaviour can have on others, eg diversity, customer service.
- When introducing a new procedure that will involve interaction with others, eg complaints procedures, appraisal schemes, disciplinary procedures.
- When you wish to reinforce theory and enable learners to see its practical application, eg health and safety.

References and Further Reading

Boal, A and Jackson, A (translator) (2002) *Games for Actors and Non-Actors*, Routledge, London

Koppett, K (2001) *Training to Imagine: Practical improvisational theatre techniques to enhance creativity, teamwork, leadership and learning*, Stylus Publishing, Sterling, VA

Koppett, K (2002) *Training Using Drama: Successful development techniques from theatre and improvisation*, Kogan Page, London

Lamont, G (2004) *The Creative Path, Living a More Vibrant Life*, Azure, London

Leigh, A and Maynard, M (2004) *Dramatic Success! Theatre techniques to transform & inspire your working life*, Nicholas Brealey Publishing, London

E-LEARNING

E-learning stands for 'electronic learning', and the term has come to replace CBT (computer-based training), CBL (computer-based learning) and multimedia learning. The CIPD define e-learning as:

> *'learning that is delivered or mediated by electronic technology for the explicit purpose of training in organizations'.*

There is some debate about whether the term covers the use of all technology such as projectors and audio/visual equipment. Here we use it to refer to learning material that is delivered and received via a network, intranet, internet or CD. It may therefore be at the learner's place of work, a learning centre or at home.

When e-learning first came into being, it tended to be about one individual studying using a computer package. With the advent of the internet and networks, e-learning can now be a group activity, giving rise to two new terms: the first is 'synchronous network', which means that learners and tutors interact with each other in real time and participate in a live electronic classroom. This may be to listen to an instructor via an audio connection or to participate in a discussion or forum. The second term, 'asynchronous network', refers to interaction that is not in real time, such as e-mails, bulletin boards etc.

E-learning was, a few years ago, going to revolutionize training and development. Companies were going to be able to reduce or lose their training departments, and have all learning pumped though computers to their staff. The reality is that this was never practical or advisable. Combining the learning and working environments is not as straightforward as it seemed – issues of noise, work priorities, equipment and staff morale need to be addressed and managed. Few people wish to learn on their own in front of a PC, and actually few people have been taught or encouraged to learn on their own. The education system in the UK encourages learning in classrooms, and consequently most of us expect to be told what to learn, when to learn and how to learn. This is reflected in the CIPD Annual Survey Report 2006, Learning and Development, which states that: 'only 1% [of respondents] believe that e-learning is the most effective way to learn'.

The idea that all learning could be given via computers was fundamentally flawed, and increasingly it is now accepted that e-learning is only effective in certain circumstances. Computer-based learning is good at conveying concepts and facts; it is particularly good for subjects such as IT (for confident users), health and safety, induction, procedures and legislation. It lends itself to bite-sized and 'just-in-time' learning. It is harder to make it work for the soft skill areas and practical skills, as these require human contact and the opportunity to practise.

Most people involved in e-learning now accept that the 'blended approach' is the key to success, mixing e-learning with tutor support and/or classroom sessions, reducing the loneliness of one learner with a computer, maximizing potential for practice and improving motivation. E-learning has a great contribution to make to training and education but only as part of an overall learning strategy. Learndirect is a government-funded initiative that uses e-learning; the learndirect website explains that:

> **learndirect** has been developed by Ufi (University for industry) with a remit from government to provide high quality post-16 learning which:
>
> - Reaches those with few or no skills and qualifications who are unlikely to participate in traditional forms of learning;
> - Equips people with the skills they need for employability, thereby strengthening the skills of the workforce and increasing productivity;
> - Is delivered innovatively through the use of new technologies.
>
> To achieve this, Ufi aims to inspire existing learners to develop their skills further, win over new and excluded learners and transform the accessibility of learning in everyday life and work.

Allesi and Trollip (2001) identified a number of possible ways in which e-learning could be used effectively:

1 tutorial mode – teaching by presenting information and guiding the learner;
2 drill mode – engaging learners in practising new knowledge or skills as a means to aiding retention and the assimilation of knowledge into long-term memory;
3 games and simulations – letting learners explore related situations;

4 assessment – testing the learner's knowledge, before, during and after using the package.

Use it because...

- *It is flexible*: the person can learn at their own pace and at a time that is convenient for them. This increases commitment to the learning as well as being highly beneficial to those who work shifts, weekends or are trying to fit their learning around other commitments such as work and family.
- *It is learner centred*: as it gives the learner control over the pace, level and sequence of learning. Learners can concentrate on the part of the course that they need. Often in a six-hour course, participants find that they already know two hours of the material and don't need the other two hours, so two-thirds of the course is a waste of time. With e-learning packages, although a learner may not finish the programme, they cover the material they need.
- *It is time effective*: it takes less time to deliver than traditional classroom methods.
- *After the start-up costs, it is cost-effective*: there are no travel or accommodation costs, and it can be used more than once.
- *It provides access to a wide range of information*: use of the internet allows the learner to find material on nearly any subject to supplement the material in the learning package.
- *Information can be presented in a variety of ways*: the use of multimedia such as graphics, audio, video and diagrams allows information to be presented in a way that is attractive to different learning styles.
- *It offers potential for a virtual classroom*: once set up, you can quickly connect people from different areas together to share experiences and knowledge.

Making it work

A key question for anyone considering introducing e-learning is whether to buy off-the-shelf packages or to have them created or tailored for their organization. The considerations here are no different than when buying a training course – you should select the one that best achieves the learning objectives and can be delivered within your budget and resource constraints. Off-the-shelf packages are often cheaper, but will not necessarily reflect your organizational culture, cover your content requirements or work on your infrastructure. Organizations creating their own material need three people to make it effective – a subject expert, an instructional designer and a programmer. A key factor to consider is how you will maintain the validity, relevance or currency of the content – if you buy off the shelf, what is the lifespan of that material? If you design your own, how easy will it be to update?

A learning management system (LMS) is the key to successful e-learning as it provides the tool for control, monitoring and evaluation. Some LMSs are expensive and complicated, requiring someone to administer them on a practically full-time basis. The key is to find an LMS that fits your organization and your e-learning strategy. Do not build an e-learning approach around an all-singing, all-dancing LMS! In selecting an LMS questions to ask are:

- How many learners will there be in total?
- How many concurrent learners will there be?
- How much tutor support do you want to have?
- What reports and information do you want?
- What other administration functions will you need?
- Who will do the administration?

E-learning can be expensive; it can also be a very cost-effective way of developing people. The following costs need to be considered when introducing e-learning:

- *Course content costs*: the purchase price, licence fees, lifetime of package and development costs.
- *Course maintenance costs*: the process and charges for updating and changing packages.
- *Hosting costs*: intranet or hosting server space and maintenance.
- *Delivery charges*: the cost of getting it to the learner, such as telecommunication and facility costs.
- *LMS costs*: software, licence, installation and customization, ongoing maintenance.
- *Hardware/infrastructure costs*: multimedia PCs, cabling, effect on help desks.
- *Tutor support*: will you have them and who will they be?
- *Administration and management costs*: who will administer user identities, passwords, reports, and user help?
- *Supporting material costs*: additional reading, manuals or handout material.
- *Consultancy costs*: initially and ongoing.

- *Collaboration*: will you have learners able to communicate with each other either on a synchronous or asynchronous basis? If so, who will monitor this communication in order to make sure it is appropriate?
- *Marketing costs*: getting the learners to use it via notices, posters, guidelines and links to other processes such as appraisal or development reviews.

Other steps that you can take to ensure e-learning is successful are:

- Have a clear e-learning policy – not just what you want to achieve, but how it will work in practice. Include sections on access to e-learning, the location of learning areas, the use of sound in open-plan offices, and relationships with other learning opportunities (blended learning).
- Secure management support, especially a sponsor who is senior within the organization. The organization and management team need to give a clear message that e-learning is encouraged and is recognized as a valid learning tool.
- Include it in the appraisal and development review process so that all members of staff are aware of the value of, and organizational approach to, learning in this way. Ensure that via these processes, specific learning objectives are established, to ensure that learners do not jump around the packages and miss the relevant learning points.
- Have an e-learning security policy in place prior to launching, which covers the use of removable disks, password security, virus protection and access to online resources.
- Try before you buy – make sure what you are buying does what you think it does and works on your delivery platforms and operating systems. Ensure that information is presented in a variety of ways and that the packages you are choosing are not just electronic books, but include some interaction by the user.
- Build it into everyday activity – require managers to allocate time for the learner to use the packages within their normal day, and to chunk and protect learning time. Build learning time into manpower plans and development plans, such as every person will have two hours' e-learning per week.
- Use pilot programmes, so that you have tested the system and packages prior to 'go-live'. One of the reasons for doing this is to ensure that they are at the right level for your learners and are not presented in a patronizing or condescending manner.
- Set up a system of champions, whose role it is to participate in the pilots, assist others and promote e-learning across the organization.

- Motivate learners – explain what is in it for them, and give them responsibility for their own learning. You could consider giving awards or prizes for using the packages and successfully completing assessments.
- Have learning pods or a learning resource centre – somewhere that learners can go away from their desks.
- Don't get seduced by the complexity, sophistication and elegance of the technology; keep it simple so it works for you.
- Have tutor and/or manager support available. People need and want the human touch. Using classroom inductions can introduce learners to the technology and to the support available to them.

It is useful for...

- Delivering knowledge-based training, eg product knowledge, systems training.
- Just-in-time or very small training sessions, such as how to solve a specific problem that exists now. For example, if someone wants to know how to do a specific thing with Excel they can go to an e-learning package and learn just that, return to their desks and implement it.
- Individuals who cannot be away from their desk for extended periods.
- Giving large, widespread organizations the opportunity to involve remote workers in learning without involving travelling and accommodation costs. Increasingly, e-learning is being used to link people from different countries in order to ensure consistency across global organizations.
- Induction – it provides the opportunity to send an introductory package via disk or internet to new people before they join the organization. (You will need to ensure that they have the necessary equipment beforehand!)
- Individuals who cannot access scheduled programmes, such as shift workers, part-time staff, night workers and weekend workers.

References and further reading

CIPD, www.cipd.co.uk/elearning

Sadler-Smith, E (2006) *Learning and Development for Managers Perspectives from research and practice*, Blackwell, Oxford

EXECUTIVE COACHING

Executive coaching is a 1:1 development method used specifically to develop senior managers and directors. It shares many of the facets of coaching in general, although it tends to focus on specific issues rather than specific skills development and the coach tends to be external to the organization. For example, an executive coach might help a managing director make decisions about a business acquisition. Increasingly, coaching professionals are identifying themselves as executive coaches, skills coaches or life coaches in order to distinguish themselves in the marketplace.

As with all coaching, the fit of coach and coachee is the key to success. Executives and senior managers will be looking for a coach who is credible and has all the skills, experience and attributes necessary to work with them. The coach must have the depth and breadth of knowledge to be able to maintain their credibility with their coachee past the initial 'sales pitch'. As executive coaching can be expensive – typical daily rates for an executive coach are £900, with some coaches charging up to £2,000 per day – it is particularly important to spend sufficient time researching options, setting objectives and selecting the right coach.

Use it because...

- Executives need development; most of the development provided by organizations is inappropriate –in terms of either content or accessibility.
- Some senior managers will have an issue with attending development events that are attended by more 'junior' staff – this is usually due to insecurities and/or company culture.
- Senior managers can often find their roles isolating and may feel unable to approach colleagues or subordinates to discuss some of the issues that they are facing. The appointment of an effective executive coach can help to alleviate some of the stress that can be caused by this isolation and provide the individual with a useful outlet for ideas and a forum for sharing thoughts and concerns.
- Senior managers have the opportunity to participate in development which is relevant to their individual needs and which can take place at a time and in a location to suit them.
- Using a coach who is external to the organization means that any potentially contentious discussions can take place in a safe and confidential

environment, without the risk of destabilizing the organization unnecessarily.

- Senior managers can receive honest feedback on their performance from an individual who is not limited by the politics of, and their position within, the organization.

Making it work

- We have already stated the importance of selecting the coach wisely; here are some of the points to look out for or consider:
  - Proven experience of coaching, supported by testimonials from previous clients that can be checked and verified.
  - The approach and methodology that the coach will use is appropriate for the individual and the organization and is ethically based; for example, will the coach agree to give open and honest feedback based upon their observations or will they tell the coachee what they think he or she wants to hear in order to keep the business? Do they baffle you with the latest 'in' technique or do they keep it simple and practical, so that even where they use a variety of techniques you have a clear understanding of why and how these will be applied?
  - Whether the coach is a member of a professional body or has accredited qualifications (this may not be important to the coachee or your organization and currently there is no regulation of this industry; there are a number of organizations and qualifications available, which, at the time of writing, do not relate to a set of national standards).
  - The rapport between the coach and the coachee – can they work together in an honest, open and constructive manner?
- There needs to be a mechanism whereby agreement is reached between the executive and the coach about the learning needs, outcomes required and measures of success. The agreement may be confidential between the coach and the coachee, depending on the reasons for the coaching taking place.
- Coaching is a relationship that has a start and a finish. To ensure that dependency does not occur, the end point should be identified at the start of the relationship. One of the selection criteria for the coach is about how they will know when the relationship can end.
- Some executive coaches do not have the relevant experience in business at a senior level and therefore are not able to fully understand the context and considerations of the situations in which the executive operates.

It is useful for...

The IES study, Inspiring Performance at Work (Carter, 2001), identified six situations when organizations may wish to engage an executive coach:

1 to support the induction of a senior person – either new to the organization or new to the role;
2 to provide accelerated personal development of 'high flyers' involved in accelerated promotion schemes or positive action schemes for minority groups;
3 to support an organizational change;
4 to provide a senior manager with a critical friend or objective sounding board;
5 to enhance other personal development programmes such as 360-degree appraisal;
6 to provide reward and recognition.

References and further reading

Berglas, S (2002) The very real dangers of executive coaching, *Harvard Business Review,* **80** (6), June, pp 86–92

Carter, A (2001) *Executive Coaching: Inspiring performance at work*, IES Report 379, Institute for Employment Studies, Brighton

MENTORING

Mentoring is the process of giving 'general advice or guidance regarding life or career' (Thorpe and Clifford, 2003). The story of Mentor is found in Homer's Odyssey; Mentor, King Odysseus' son's trusted friend, adviser, and teacher, is the name given to those people who help us move towards our goals and reach our potential.

Mentoring is different from coaching, which is the process of helping an individual enhance or improve a specific skill in order to improve their performance. Mentoring covers a range of issues, and therefore is more general than coaching. Traditionally, a mentor is often someone who is senior to the learner, either within an organization or within their specialist field, and who can offer help or advice on how the organization/industry works, give support for the learner, share their experiences, encourage professional behaviour, explore options and assist with the learner's career. In recent years, criticism of sponsorship by senior executives and concerns over favouritism mean that seniority and organizational position are less important now than having mentors who are more experienced, have greater expertise, and who have the skills to help the learner develop.

Gordon F Shea, in his book *Mentoring: A guide to the basics* (1992), offers seven types of mentor assistance:

- helping a person to shift her or his mental context;
- listening when the mentoree has a problem;
- identifying mentoree feelings and verifying them (feedback);
- effectively confronting negative intentions or behaviour;
- delegating authority or giving permission;
- providing appropriate information when needed;
- encouraging exploration of options.

In order to do this, a mentor will need to be able to:

- listen effectively;
- confront positively;
- envisage outcomes;
- make observations;
- explain how to get things done in or through the organization;
- set parameters and boundaries for the relationship;
- identify feelings and issues;
- communicate information;
- encourage and motivate;
- give feedback;
- ask appropriate questions.

Mentoring relationships can exist for a long time, and may be formal or informal. Some organizations have formal mentoring schemes; others rely on individuals to find their own mentor. Some professional bodies provide lists of their experienced members who can provide this support. Some individuals discover that their mentor is someone with whom they are friends, rather than having a formal mentoring agreement.

Use it because…

- It provides a role model for the learner; someone from whom they can gain examples of appropriate behaviour in different situations, or who can advise them on what to do or not do in various scenarios.

- The learner has an objective person in whom they can confide, and with whom they can share their hopes and fears. This may be to ask that 'silly question' that they don't feel able to ask their manager or colleague, or to explore 'what ifs' in order to hone their thinking and make their own decisions.
- Experience and standards can be passed down to a new person, which provides consistency and congruence.
- It is not resource intensive, which makes it cost-effective.

Making it work

- For a formal mentoring scheme, ensure that the mentors are selected against stated criteria and are trained if necessary in appropriate interpersonal skills. Some mentors are not able to communicate well with learners – they have been chosen because of their experience or specialism, but lack the interpersonal skills needed to be effective.
- Be clear on the purpose of mentoring and what you want to achieve by having it. Some mentors are tied too much to the past and their own experiences to be useful to the leaner. This may mean that, consciously or subconsciously, they sabotage attempts to introduce change into an organization, or criticize new thinking. Equally, if they are feeling negative about what is happening, this might be transferred to the learner.
- Ensure that time to meet is prioritized by both the mentor and the mentoree. It will fail if meetings are rushed or there are long gaps between meetings.
- Give responsibility for agenda setting to the learner, so that they can address or discuss areas that are important and relevant to them, as well as take ownership of their learning.

It is useful for...

- Individuals who have a specialist knowledge, who need to extend their understanding of the organization or another field.
- New people joining a large organization who will benefit from having advice on 'how things work' around here.
- High flyers, who are seen as part of the succession plans.
- Staff undertaking a graduate or competency scheme.
- Supporting a professional CPD scheme.

References and further reading

Hay, J (1999) *Transformational Mentoring*, Sherwood Publishing, Watford

Parsloe, E (1999) *The Manager as Coach and Mentor*, 2nd edn, CIPD, London

Shea, G F (1992) *Mentoring: A guide to the basics*, Kogan Page, London

NETWORKING

The process of networking is renowned as a marketing technique for getting new business. In its broadest sense it is about making links and connections with other people in order to share knowledge, skills and ideas, and this makes it an ideal development tool. Networking can take place formally or informally, it can be within or outside one's own organization and it can be face-to-face or electronic.

Much networking can take place via membership of professional bodies and special interest groups. We discuss the uses of professional membership later in this chapter.

Most people who have been able to achieve within their own organizations have an innate ability to network; that is, they have developed relationships with a band of people whom they know and trust and whom they can contact to help them solve a problem, check out information, or achieve a task. Very successful people generally utilize their contacts outside as well as inside their existing organization. (See Figure 4.1 for an example of a personal network.)

Use it because...

- It enables the individual to access specialists and other knowledgeable people to help them achieve their learning objectives and goals.
- It can provide access to information about what others are doing, potential changes and developments in functional areas, latest thinking etc.
- Networking provides the opportunity for a person to see how others behave and to learn from these observations.
- It opens up opportunities for career movement and/or secondments as it enables the person to show others what they are like and to discuss their capabilities without the pressure of interviews or deadlines.

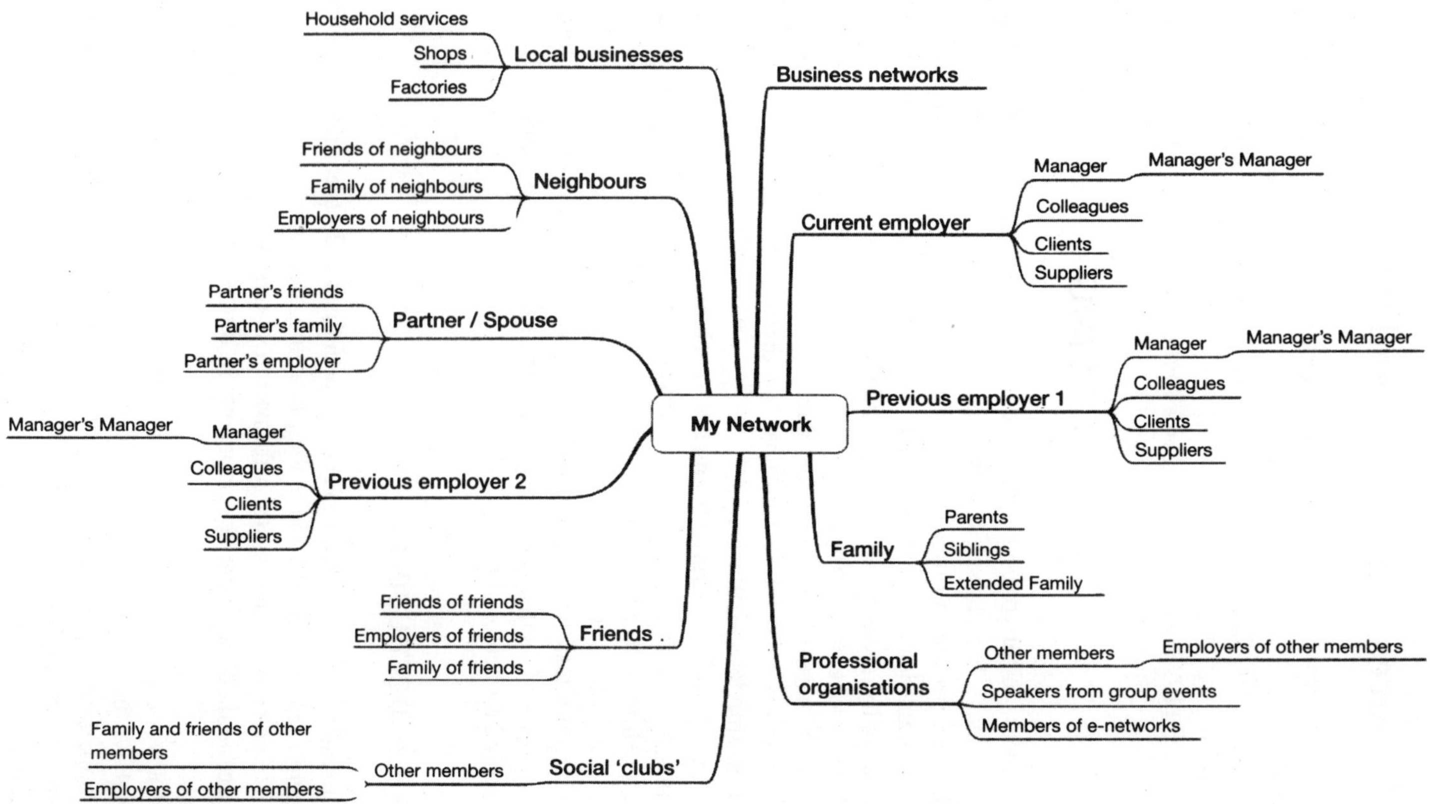

Figure 4.1 A personal network

- Networking is an opportunity to make and receive qualified referrals and contacts, which could be useful in the future should other problems or issues arise.
- Networking is ideal for developing interpersonal skills in an experiential way, such as turning the conversation towards business, breaking into a group, extracting yourself from conversations, showing interest, listening etc.
- It is cost-effective and can combine individual development with gaining new business.
- It tends to occur outside normal working hours, such as breakfast, lunch and evening meetings, and therefore has less impact on the working day.

Making it work

Most of the information available about networking gives advice on using it as a marketing tool. Below are the key principles of using this technique, placing the focus on learning and development, which you may want to give to the learner:

- Consider your learning and development goals. What are you trying to achieve? What will help you? Think about specific skills that you are trying to develop.
- Attend a variety of different events and meetings, internally and externally. Choose the events you are going to attend sensibly. Will they help you meet your learning objectives? Is the subject relevant? Will the other attendees have something to offer you on the area that you want to learn?
- Plan before you attend. Who do you want to meet? Can you identify a specific outcome that you will gain from each meeting? If more than one of you in your team are attending the event, have a team plan so that you are networking widely.
- Talk to people you don't know and have less contact with those you do know. This will allow you to widen your network as far as possible. Avoid the 'comfort trap' of only talking to people you know or to your colleagues.
- Avoid talking to one person for too long at one event. Have a maximum of 10 minutes with each person you meet.
- Actively listen – remember the 'magnificent 7 questions' of 'who', 'what', 'why', 'which', 'when', 'where', and 'how'. This will give you clues to how you can help them, and how they can help you. Show genuine interest in what they have to say.

- Be able to describe your business and what you do in 60 seconds – try to give more than just a job title as this won't give the person very much information about you and your skills.
- Ask questions that link to your learning objectives. Has the person you are talking to experience in...? What are their thoughts on...?
- Exchange business cards with those you meet whenever this is appropriate. Write comments on the back of the business cards you collect – it helps you remember whom you met and where.
- Think about what you can offer them as well as what they can offer you so that information exchange is a two-way process.
- Follow up and contact the people you meet. Be aware that you may not always be able to use the information that you get immediately, but reflection and maintaining ongoing relationships will enable you to build up an information store for the future.
- Review afterwards. Did you meet your objectives? What skills did you use during the event? Were you happy with how you behaved or performed? What would you do differently with the benefit of hindsight? What's your plan now? Watch out for unexpected benefits or learning – those that weren't planned but are worthy of noting.

Other considerations to ensure networking is effective are:

- Ensure management buy in to networking as a development tool, which will overcome the argument that it is a jolly away from work.
- Choose events carefully to meet the learner's objectives, rather than just attend for the sake of attending. You cannot guarantee who the learner will come across within the networking group and therefore they may not always get the information that they want or need. So encourage them to research and ask existing members of the group about who goes and what happens.

It is useful for...

- Individuals who need to enhance their social, interpersonal or meeting skills.
- Senior managers to widen their general business knowledge.
- Small organizations that only have one or two people doing a specific function.
- Professionals such as lawyers, HR professionals, accountants and engineers, who can discuss their experiences for others to learn from.

- High-technology or rapidly changing industries, as it is a good way of keeping in touch with the latest developments.
- Individuals who do not receive regular updates via their own internal organizations, either because they are a specialist function or because communication is poor.

References and further reading

Hart, R (1996) *Effective Networking for Professional Success*, Kogan Page, London

Misner, I R (1994) *The World's Best Known Marketing Secret: Building your business with word of mouth marketing*, Bard & Stephen, Austin, TX

Wilson, J R (1991) *Word of Mouth Marketing*, John Wiley & Sons, Chichester

ON-THE-JOB TRAINING

On-the-job training (OJT), also called workplace instruction or 'sitting by Nellie', is one of the oldest and most common forms of workplace learning. Done properly, it is structured training which takes place in the workplace (on the job) on a 1:1 basis, with the appointed 'instructor' showing the learner how to do a task. The appointed instructor is usually a more experienced colleague, although they can be a supervisor, buddy, 'floor-walker' or designated line trainer. The CIPD Annual Survey Report 2006, Learning and Development, states that 'almost 4 in 10 respondents say that on-the-job training is the most effective form of learning in their organization'. This makes it the most effective method of development identified by this survey.

OJT is highly valid and relevant to the learner – it occurs in a real environment with real work, and as such provides the learner with a realistic experience and opportunity to apply or transfer their learning straightaway. Many organizations do not monitor their OJT and therefore it is difficult to assess how much this is used, although it is widely estimated that there is at least a 50/50 split between on- and off-the-job training. Research shows that OJT tends to be focused at process or operative learning; it can be very useful for managerial training which is often delivered via formal off-the-job courses.

Use it because...

- Work is still being done, albeit maybe more slowly, whilst training is taking place.
- OJT can be tailored to meet the learning style of the individual being trained and can also take place at a pace dictated by the individual's needs and abilities.
- People are learning how to do a job in the setting in which it takes place and are therefore subject to the same pressures and environmental influences as they will be when they are performing the task for real, and therefore the learning has maximum face validity.
- It can take place at a time to suit all parties involved and can be rescheduled at short notice.
- Evidence of competence is more readily available, as the learner does the job or task there and then. Equally, poor performance or difficulties can be identified and overcome earlier and before they become habits.
- OJT is cost-effective for the organization because it utilizes existing resources and can be a development tool, not only for the trainee, but also the trainer. As it occurs in the workplace, learning is faster and more effective, resulting in trainees becoming fully productive more quickly.
- Quite often the instructor is on the spot if the trainee has questions after the training has taken place.

Making it work

The CIPD Guide to On-the-job Training (1997) identifies seven simple steps to effective job OJT or instruction:

1. A supervisor or experienced colleague shows a worker how to perform a task.
2. They explain to the worker the key points about the task.
3. They perform the task again with the learner watching.
4. The learner performs simple parts of the task, with the instructor watching.
5. The instructor helps the worker perform the whole job.
6. The learner performs the whole task or job with the instructor watching and providing feedback.
7. The learner now performs the task on their own.

In order to make this seven-step process effective, take into account the following:

- Consider if OJT is appropriate – to what is being learnt, the environment and your organization's culture. For example, whilst it can be good to learn in the place where the job is carried out, this may be inappropriate if it is noisy, dirty or unsafe.
- Select the trainers/instructors for their skills and ability to show others how to do something – not just because they have the time, need a new challenge, want a new job or deserve recognition. Consider the fact that the person who is the most skilled may not always be the person who will be the best OJ trainer.
- Use colleagues rather than superiors – this removes the learner's blocks and their fear of being assessed, thus providing a safer and more productive learning environment.
- Train the trainers/instructors and give them support from training professionals. Basic training for trainers must include, as a minimum, how adults learn, learning styles, demonstration skills, use of questions, how to give feedback, planning and design of learning sessions, and assessing achievement.
- Think about your quality assurance procedures. How will you monitor the people selected to 'train'? How will you know if they are doing the task itself properly and that they will not pass on bad habits or unacceptable short cuts? What will you do if they are not doing the job properly? How will you ensure that they are training properly?
- Consider integrating it with other forms of development, such as e-learning, self-study or training courses – this allows knowledge to be learnt away from the workplace, and focuses OJT onto transference and application of skills.
- Ensure your OJT covers the 'why' and not just the 'how' – not doing this may result in little understanding of the bigger picture or the consequences and impact of what they are doing. This can in turn lead to the learner making unacceptable short cuts because processes seem unnecessary to them, or they are not aware of dependencies later in the process. Understanding where 'I' fit in links to improved motivation and sense of well-being, as well as improving team working.
- Reward your trainers – either financially or with an alternative recognition such as a revised job title and description.
- Accept that whilst the job will get done, it will be done at a slower pace. Therefore build this into your targets and manpower plans and utilize slack times for training.

- Record who has been trained, what they covered, for how long and who trained them, so this can be recognized as part of the development budget and commitment.
- Give the trainers the opportunity to get together regularly to share experiences and ideas.
- Provide backup material for the learners such as procedure documents, method statements, safe systems of work, and handouts.

It is useful for…

- Inducting new employees.
- A process-driven or procedural-driven role/organization.
- Repetitive tasks or for irregular tasks.
- Very specialist tasks where other methods may not be available.
- In a handover situation.

Reference and further reading

Cannell, M (1997) *The IPD Guide to On-the-Job Training*, CIPD, London

OUTDOOR EDUCATION/LEARNING

Outdoor training or education appears to have different definitions to different people, from those who view it as education about nature and the 'out-of-doors' world, to those who advocate adventurous sports as a method for achieving work-related development of teams and individuals. The Outdoor Institute defines outdoor education as 'the use of experiences in the outdoors for the education and development of the "whole person"'. James Neill, one of the leading writers to be found in this area, summarizes it as 'Outdoor education is a term that means different things to different people, cultures, and organizations. Common themes include an emphasis on direct experience of the outdoors for personal, social, educational, therapeutic and environmental goals' (Neill, 2003).

Generally outdoor learning involves groups of people carrying out adventurous activities or tasks in order to learn new or enhanced skills, knowledge and attitudes. It is therefore most often used, but not exclusively, for the development of management, communication, interpersonal and problem-solving skills. Outdoor activities vary greatly, from a short team-building exercise or a walk in the woods to survival challenges.

In choosing the activity it is extremely important to consider the group and the individuals within the group in terms of their physical and mental capacity to cope with such challenges. Whilst putting someone into a real or perceived survival situation can result in increasing skills and confidence, it can also have the converse effect.

Used effectively, outdoor development takes individuals out of their natural setting and requires them to use their skills (known or unknown) in a new way. This can accelerate learning because it brings the skills into focus and offers the opportunity for prolonged reflection. Outdoor learning appeals to all the senses – visual, audio, taste, touch and smell, and as such, experiences become more powerful and intense.

In 1997, Priest and Gass proposed four purposes of adventure programmes:

1. recreational: the purpose being leisure, fun and enjoyment resulting in a change in the way people feel;
2. educational: to learn new skills or information (remember the school field trips!);
3. developmental: where the purpose is to undergo some personal growth, such as increasing self-esteem, building self-discipline and testing endurance;
4. therapeutic/redirectional: programmes that aim to correct an individual by working on the way they think, behave, feel and resist. This, for example, could be used with offenders in order to prepare them to rejoin society.

James Neill suggested four additions to these purposes:

1. Spiritual – the purpose of which is to develop spiritual knowledge and experience.
2. Relationship/family – which aims to change the way a particular group is functioning and interacting.
3. Community – the purpose of which is to change the way a group feels and behaves. This differs from therapeutic purposes as it focuses on the group rather than an individual.
4. Environmental – programmes which have goals aimed at supporting the natural environment as opposed to supporting humans.

In adult development, any of these purposes may be valid, although the purposes of education, development, relationship and community are most obviously linked to workplace learning.

The CIPD has produced guidance on selecting outdoor activity providers and on the safety aspects that must be considered. It may also be of interest that under the 1995 The Activities Centres (Young Persons' Safety) Act, all centres offering activities to young people, and who operate in a commercial manner (not voluntary organizations), are required to be licensed by the Adventurous Activities Licensing Authority, which inspects providers on behalf of the Department of Education and Skills.

Use it because...

- Being outdoors encourages the use of all the senses and as such provides a more powerful or complete experience, from which the learner can draw conclusions and learning. It promotes multi-sensory learning and can therefore accelerate the learning process.
- Participants have the opportunity to use their skills and knowledge in what is, for most, a completely different setting from normal. This enables them to see if their usual behaviours work, and to consider how to change or enhance them to make them more effective in this new setting. Consider a manager who only communicates via e-mail or in 1:1 settings, who now has to get his team building a raft – different communication techniques need to be employed and practised.
- It engages the participants on an emotional level; whether they like or hate being outside, it is impacting upon their emotions and engaging their limbic system, one of the oldest parts of the brain. This is of benefit because the memory of the experience will be much deeper, and therefore the learning will be greater.
- There is a huge variety of activities that can be used, offering choice and flexibility to tailor the learning event to the needs and learning styles of the participants.
- Being outside can have a big impact on people's sense of well-being, and therefore puts them in the right frame of mind for learning.
- The weather, and nature! We can't control everything, yet large parts of our working lives are spent trying to! Taking into account the incontrollable, such as beating rain or burning sunshine, adds a dimension to learning situations that is very hard to simulate or totally plan for.

Making it work

- *Complete a cost-benefit analysis.* Outdoor learning can be expensive and you need to weigh up the predicted learning outcomes against the costs of running an event. You will need to take into account the cost of health and safety implications, the costs of residential accommodation, the equipment costs and the cost of a good facilitator.

- *Be clear on your purpose.* Why are you using the outdoors? Is this the best learning method? If the event is a 'jolly' that's fine, but be clear that the only expected outcome is that people enjoy themselves.
- *Select the outdoor activity with care.* Sometimes outdoor activities are suggested because of the facilitator's preference rather than because they will meet the learning need. There is no point going outside for the sake of being outside; the activity must add value to the event and support the achievement of the learning objectives. Some people dislike the out-of-doors and physical activity, and forcing them to participate would be inappropriate. Therefore it is important to consider who the learners will be, their preferences and how challenging you can be before planning this type of activity.
- *Select facilitators who can draw out the learning.* A potential problem is that the facilitator is a specialist in the activity and is unable to 'unpack' the experience, meaning that learning is not identified or action plans for changing behaviours are not properly drawn up. It is important to have a facilitator or facilitators who can lead the activity *and* handle the feedback and follow-up sessions.
- *Build in time to reflect on workplace application.* This type of event has immediate impact, but unless followed up with consideration of the practical implementation of the learning, the learning will not be embedded. It is vital that learning gained via this type of experiential learning is drawn out properly and fully.

It is useful for...

- Outdoor learning and development is particularly good for team working, communications, problem solving, decision making, creativity, leadership and project management skills. It is also excellent at promoting learning at an affective level – development that requires reviews of values and beliefs.

References and further reading

Neill J, www.wilderdon.com

Priest, S and Gass, M (1997), *Effective Leadership in Adventure Programming*, Human Kinetics, Champaign, IL

PROFESSIONAL MEMBERSHIP

Membership of an institute, association or organization set up specifically for people who have common work or professional interests can be a valuable development tool. A Google search for 'professional institutes' in the UK produced a list of approximately 908,000 websites. We are unable to list them all, suffice to say that there appears to be an organization or group for most occupations and interests.

Many of the institutes and organizations appear to have similar purposes – the promotion of that occupational field, the setting and maintenance of professional standards, and services to members. Some also provide licences or authority to act within an area of work.

As a development tool, professional membership of these institutes provides knowledge by updating members on current thinking, detailing changes to law, organizing networking groups, providing access to libraries, member events, experts and websites. Most provide training courses and several have professional qualifications linked to their levels of membership. An increasing number of professions have the requirement for continuing professional development (CPD), which can be achieved by attending accredited events. Others are more informal and require members to show continuous development but do not audit or dictate what and where it has to be taken.

Membership of professional bodies can be paid for by an organization or the individual themselves, and similarly some organizations give time off to attend events. For some, membership subscriptions are tax deductible.

Use it because...

- Being part of such a body provides access to information that might not enter your employing organization by any other means – for example, planned changes by government or new legislation – and this is particularly important for specialists who are working in isolation.
- It gives the opportunity for individuals to enhance expertise or widen their knowledge of one element of their profession by liaising with, participating in or supporting specialist interest groups.
- Learners gain access to professional and specialist resources – surveys, websites, libraries, legal lines, experts.
- Achieving professional recognition and status can enhance career prospects and be an indicator of competence.

- Individuals can network across their functional specialism rather than their company's sector. For example, an HR manager working within manufacturing can network with other HR managers via the Chartered Institute of Personnel and Development (CIPD).
- There may be a ready-made competency or continuing professional development (CPD) scheme which will encourage ongoing development and learning.
- Members of professional bodies can often access training courses on specialist subjects at a reduced rate.

Making it work

- Help the learner to establish a clear purpose for wanting to join a professional body. Often individuals are confused about which institute or body to join – do they join the most well known or the one that best serves their needs as a specialist within this industry?
- You need to have a clear organizational policy about the importance that is placed upon professional membership for staff in different grades and roles. This policy must also state how the organization intends to support professional membership – this could be financially, by allowing time off to attend meetings or by supporting events. A policy such as this will prevent a person from spending all their time at events or professional body meetings rather than working, which leads both colleagues and employers to question the purpose of membership.
- Help the learner to contextualize information that they have gathered from their professional body in order to make it relevant to your organization.

It is useful for...

- Individuals who are technically competent, but need to widen their knowledge of the general profession or update themselves on the wider context of their work.
- Succession and organizational development planning as you may want to ask individuals to achieve certain levels of membership of professional bodies.
- Graduates to further their industry-specific or specialist knowledge.
- Areas that are subject to a large amount of legislation change.

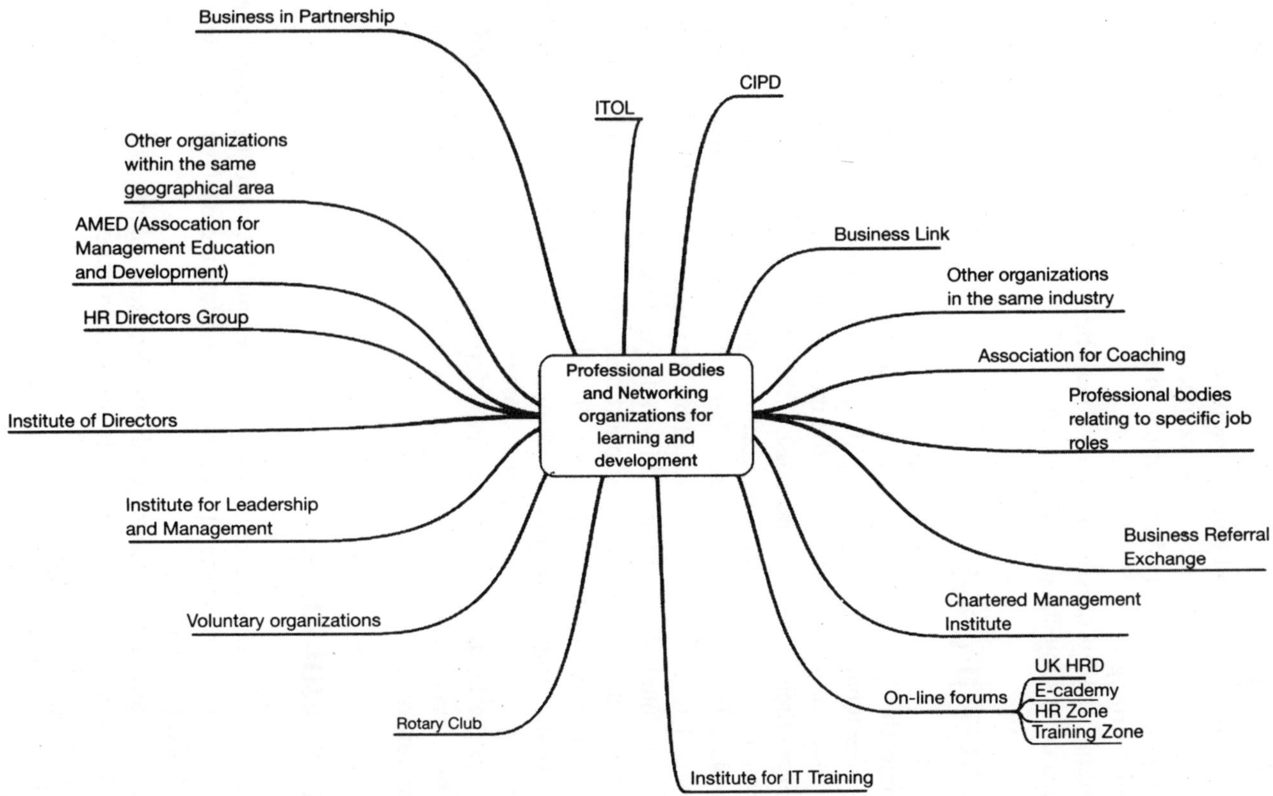

Figure 4.2 A network of professional bodies for a learning and development specialist

PROFESSIONAL SUPERVISION

Supervision is a structured, reflective process which focuses on professional decisions, actions and outcomes. It is most often used in the health and social care sectors but has been utilized in other professions such as engineering, training and more recently coaching. The main characteristic is that it is an ongoing process as opposed to coaching which has a start and finish point. It is different from mentoring in that it follows a structured approach rather than being ad hoc. In terms of learning outcomes it will not have specific learning outcomes as it focuses on what is currently happening and what can be learnt from it.

There are very many definitions of supervision; the one offered by the Department of Health seems to encompass the main themes:

> *A formal process of professional support and learning which enables individual practitioners to develop knowledge and competence, assume responsibility for their own practice and enhance consumer protection and safety of care in complex clinical situations. It is central to the process of learning and to the scope of the expansion of practice and should be seen as a means of encouraging self-assessment and analytical and reflective skills (Vision for the future 1993).*

Supervision is not a disciplinary process; it should not be used by either the supervisor or the supervisee as a route to air complaints or have a 'general moan'. Julie Hay in *Train the Trainer* notes that: 'within industry supervision customarily means someone who checks your work, tells you what to do... in the helping professions, it has a distinctly different meaning, referring to someone who helps you to "review" your work so that you see things differently.'

When used effectively, supervision is a true opportunity to implement reflective practice and therefore can be applied to many settings, not only those related to health or social care. Any manager who wishes to provide ongoing support and development for his or her team members can use the process of supervision to do so.

Use it because...

When used effectively, supervision provides the opportunity to:

- reflect upon working activities within an open and honest environment;
- consider future learning and development needs;
- discuss ways in which to continuously improve;
- identify and share good practice;
- take a step back and think creatively through a range of issues and problems;
- advocate peer support through peer supervision that can often be more effective than manager-led supervision because the risk of straying into disciplinary and performance management issues is taken away.

Making it work

If you have decided to implement a supervision process, the following points will be useful to remember:

1. The team and individuals who are going to be involved in supervising and being supervised should understand and agree to be part of the process.
2. Supervision meetings should be viewed as confidential meetings where there will be an opportunity to discuss incidents and events, share best practice and participate in an open and honest dialogue about what is currently happening within the workplace.
3. Participants in the process should be encouraged to develop skills in active listening and effective questioning in order to gain most benefit.
4. The process of supervision should be defined and followed in every meeting. Each meeting should have a beginning, middle and end and should be recorded in a way that is agreed by the participants.
5. A method for evaluating the success of the process should be agreed upon.

Whilst supervision can be a very effective tool for development, there are also a number of risks attached to it, which you need to be aware of in order to minimize their impact. These risks are:

- Where the participants in the process do not have faith in, for example, the confidentiality aspects, they will not feel able to be honest and therefore will not take part fully.
- The process will not suit all individuals. Many people feel that it is simply a 'navel-gazing' exercise and therefore become frustrated at

what they see as pointless discussion, when they could be getting on with their work.

- The process is time consuming and is not practical when a supervisor is a line manager responsible for a large team. Meetings should be limited to a maximum of one hour so that they are focused and productive.
- The process can be draining for the supervisor and therefore measures must be put in place for the supervisor themselves to have supervision.

It is useful for...

- Individuals whose job roles involve them in difficult situations involving clients or customers; for example, dealing with complaints, processing difficult applications, giving bad news. In these situations, supervision provides the opportunity to offload and review within a work setting; this can be of great benefit to the well-being of staff and can be part of the process of achieving a good work–life balance. This is why supervision is most often used in health and social care settings.
- Supervision does not work for individuals whose roles involve repetitive tasks. It works best for those who are working in customer/client-facing roles or who face a series of 'critical incidents' on a daily basis.

References and further reading

www.clinical-supervision.com This website deals with supervision in a clinical situation, but can provide some useful information for those who wish to adapt this process for use in different settings

Hawkins, P and Shohet, R (2000) *Supervision in the Helping Professions*, 2nd edn, Open University Press, Maidenhead

Proctor, B (1986) Supervision: a co-operative exercise in accountability, in *Enabling and Ensuring: Supervision in practice*, ed A Marken and N Payne, Leicester National Youth Bureau/Council for Education and Training in Youth and Community Work, Leicester

PROJECTS

This is where a learner is placed, part or full time, into an acknowledged project within an organization, as part of their development plan. A project has a start and a finish, with specific objectives, terms of reference and required outcomes.

By joining the project team, the learner is required to use their skills, knowledge and/or approaches differently in order to achieve the requirements of the project. Invariably they are required to work with people with whom they don't regularly work, which provides the opportunity for much learning around interpersonal skills. Whilst ideally project teams are made up of people who have all the skills and experience the project requires, this is not always possible without additional outside recruitment. In organizations with tight budgets or headcounts, the lack of authority to recruit may mean that the existing team members have to learn brand-new skills and assume new responsibilities to account for gaps within the team – an ideal development ground and alternative to other learning methods.

Use it because...

- The learner is able to develop or enhance their existing skills and knowledge whilst carrying out a real piece of work – this means that the learning has excellent validity and relevancy, enabling the learner to embed it to a deeper level.
- It combines technical knowledge with softer or business skill areas such as communication, team working and management skills. Increasingly, organizations are seeing that this is more beneficial as it presents a holistic approach to learning rather than splitting up these two distinct aspects of performance (technical and business/personal skills). This latter approach can result in learners struggling to combine the two areas within their roles at work.
- Project team members are often from different backgrounds, work specialisms and interests, which provides the opportunity for individuals to increase their knowledge and understanding of these, as well as awareness of how others view the same situation.

Making it work

- Have a realistic time management and resource allocation plan to ensure that there is a balance between project work and 'day job'.
- Don't just throw the learner in at the deep end; analyse their starting point in terms of their current skills and knowledge against what they will need to fulfil their role in the project team. They need to have the baseline skills to start with, which may require some form of training before the project begins.

- Provide ongoing support for the learner. Don't forget that the learner is participating in the project in order to develop, so whilst the project manager will review their work performance, you or their line manager need to monitor progress against their development plan. Teams focusing on the objectives of the project could overlook the requirements of individual team members, and therefore the learning could be damaged.
- Poorly performing project teams can disrupt the project and the individual's learning plan.

It is useful for...

- Developing individuals through a very practical method – learning by doing. We have identified three occasions when a project can be used as a development tool:
  1. A piece of work that needs doing and is given to someone to stretch them and develop them.
  2. An organizational project to which the individual will actively add because of their expertise or skills and in the course of doing so will develop an aspect of themselves – this is good for specialists who need to learn about other aspects of the business. Also, this is very good for individuals who need to learn how to interact with other people.
  3. Joining a project team to fill a gap in individual experience such as managing a team or project – sending an individual to a project so that they can fill the gap is especially useful to fulfil CPD requirements. This is also a good test of how competent someone is.
- Projects are a very effective development method because the person is learning by doing and getting feedback from a variety of sources. They work especially well for soft-skills learning such as negotiation, communication and team working. The structured nature of projects means that they provide a framework within which development can take place.
- When basic skills have already been attained, projects give the learner the opportunity to apply those skills in a real-life situation, which appeals to activists and pragmatists.
- Working on a project can assist with someone's profile across departments or the organization, so that others outside their own department can see their abilities.
- Being involved with a project is obviously good at increasing project management skills – even as a project team member, an individual will

learn a lot about running projects, including processes, terminology, interfacing with stakeholders and reviewing.

QUALIFICATIONS

In this section we discuss academic and vocational qualifications. As with any of the methods that are listed in this chapter, the choice of type of qualification will depend upon the required outcomes of the development. Academic qualifications are more applicable to situations where learners need to develop knowledge and critical-thinking skills, whereas vocational qualifications provide evidence of competence in practical skills. Another decision to be made is whether to offer in-house or nationally recognized qualifications. The following questions will support the decision-making process:

- Do we want the learner to develop knowledge or skills?
- Why do we need the learners to achieve a qualification – what benefit will this have for us as an organization?
- Is it important for the learner to meet national standards?
- Do we have our own in-house standards to which the learner must work – how do these relate to the national standards?
- Do we wish to develop an accredited in-house programme? Are we willing to go through the accreditation processes of an external body, eg Institute of Leadership and Management (ILM)?
- Are we happy to offer an in-house certificated programme that is not externally moderated or transferable between organizations?
- How important is it for the learner to have a certificate with our own 'branding' or a certificate from a national awarding body, eg City and Guilds or Edexcel?
- How well do the curricula for the nationally recognized qualifications relate to our business requirements for these learners?

Academic qualifications

Academic qualifications are qualifications which are knowledge based and generally involve an assessment process based upon examinations, essay writing and/or coursework. In contrast to vocational qualifications, they focus on what an individual knows as opposed to what they can do.

Academic qualifications enable individuals to develop and demonstrate analytical and critical skills and, if studied whilst working full or part time, they demonstrate time-management and planning skills as well as a commitment to ongoing personal development. Higher-level academic qualifications demonstrate higher-level skills in reasoning, presenting arguments and in complex thinking.

Academic qualifications can be gained by full- or part-time study. Depending upon the nature and level of the qualification, they can be studied at further education colleges, universities and via distance learning. Most qualifications are taught, but at higher levels qualifications can be gained through research.

Use it because...

- Studying an academic qualification can give an individual time away from their workplace which can provide an opportunity to reflect on their own performance and consider ways in which it might be improved.
- Most academic qualifications involve written work; learners will not only develop their knowledge in the chosen subject area, but will also develop their written communication skills.
- Gaining a recognized qualification can provide a significant boost in confidence which in turn can lead to improved performance.
- Studying at an academic institution can provide good networking opportunities and access to new and different sources of information.
- Gaining an academic qualification is a requirement for some fields and professions. The achievement of the qualification indicates a certain status, degree of professionalism and/or level of knowledge and may be linked to the job grade and remuneration that the individual can expect.

Making it work

- *Allocate time.* Individuals will need to take time away from their workplace if they are studying at an institution full or part time. If they are studying out of working time or via distance learning, they may request time back or they may become resentful of the time that they are using in order to study. There is also an issue with the length of time it takes to achieve the qualification. Studying for an academic qualification not only requires time to be allocated to attend college or work at home, it also requires time for revision and examinations.
- *Select the appropriate level.* The level of course which an individual is studying should be challenging, but achievable. If the course that you

select is too easy or, conversely, too difficult, the learner may become bored or demotivated. The academic institution providing the course should be able to provide advice and guidance about appropriate levels of study, including entry requirements and an initial assessment of ability/current knowledge.

- *Provide support – personally and technically.* Academic courses are demanding and the learner may require help with the content and/or access to technical knowledge. They may also need some personal support when the going gets difficult. In many cases assessment takes place at the end of the course and you will need to put in place plans to provide additional support when the results are communicated because if the learner does not pass, they may be upset or angry and they may not be able to progress to the next year of their course.
- *Help learners deal with exam nerves.* Some individuals find taking examinations hugely stressful. This is particularly relevant for individuals who have not taken exams for some time or who did not succeed in previous exams. Pressure may be increased if the qualification is a requirement of the employer or the individual's professional body. This may result in a drop in performance levels at work/on the course and you may observe symptoms of stress such as increased illness or changes in personality and behaviour. To combat this, find a way to provide learners with some general study skills and exam techniques either via the learning provider or in the workplace.
- *Agree the purpose of the course.* Academic qualifications are curriculum driven and therefore the learning may not be applicable to the job and/or the organization. Exam-based academic qualifications prove that the individual has the ability to recall facts for an exam, but they do not necessarily mean that the knowledge will be remembered in the future or can be applied in the 'real world'. Therefore, have the conversation with the manager and the learner about why studying this qualification will benefit them and the organization, including how the learning will be applied in the workplace.
- *Have a sponsorship policy.* This policy should include what courses you will support and the level of funding available. It should also state what will happen if individuals do not pass exams or assessments at the first attempt or decide to withdraw from the course. You can include other support that is on offer, such as expenses, study leave and access to experts within the organization.

It is useful for...

- Theorists, who will thrive if they are offered an academic qualification. Many theorists will see this as a reward for the work that they have done.
- Reflectors, who will also find benefit in working towards an academic qualification as it will give them the opportunity to think about what they are learning and how it relates to their day-to-day work.
- Some professions (such as accountancy, medicine, teaching and law), which require qualifications that can only be gained via the academic route.
- Some technical jobs, where a large amount of theoretical knowledge is required which is best gained through an academic qualification, for example engineering or architecture. Passing an exam proves that an individual has the required knowledge at the point of taking the exam.
- Organizations where academic recognition is important. In some organizations a manager will not be able to progress without achieving an MBA.
- Organizations that wish to develop the intellectual capacity and capability of their employees and therefore develop the intellectual capacity of the organization, if the learning is applied back in the workplace.

Vocational qualifications

Vocational training in its broadest sense is training which prepares an individual to take up a specific trade, career or profession. Vocational qualifications provide certification to demonstrate that an individual has achieved a stated level of competence in their chosen field; these can be developed in-house or be part of the national framework.

The following paragraphs focus on NVQs (National Vocational Qualifications) and briefly outline what can be a very complex and confusing world for those who are not working with it on a daily basis. We hope that this information is useful and provides some insight into the language and variety of organizations that are involved in delivering vocational qualifications.

In the UK there is a range of vocational qualifications available; these qualifications fall under the supervision of the relevant regulatory authorities, all formed in 1997.

In England the regulatory authority is the Qualifications and Curriculum Authority (QCA). The QCA came from the merger of the National Council for Vocational Qualifications (NCVQ) and the School Curriculum and Assessment Authority (SCAA).

It is the role of the QCA to monitor standards in education and training in England. The QCA has the responsibility for the development of a coherent framework and the accreditation of school, college and work-based qualifications. This framework is known as the National Qualifications Framework (NQF) and has a number of levels within it.

The NQF now has eight levels, rather than the original five. There is also a framework for Higher Education Qualifications (HFEQ). See Table 4.1.

The Scottish Qualifications Authority (SQA) combines the functions of the former Scottish Examination Board (SEB) and SCOTVEC. Other than for degrees and professional qualifications, SQA is the sole body responsible for Scottish Qualifications. It is also responsible for the accreditation of SVQs (Scottish Vocational Qualifications) and provides advice to the Scottish Executive on Scottish qualifications.

The regulatory authority for Wales is the ACCAC (Awdurdod Cymwysterau, Cwricwlwm Ac Asesu Cymru/Qualifications, Curriculum and Assessment Authority for Wales). Also formed in 1997 by the merger of the Curriculum and Assessment Authority for Wales (ACAC) and the NCVQ (Wales office), the ACCAC regulates all external qualifications in Wales except for NVQs, which remain within the responsibility of the QCA.

Table 4.1

National Qualifications Framework		**Framework for Higher Education Qualifications**
Previous Levels	**Current Levels**	**Levels**
Level 5	Level 8	D (doctoral)
	Level 7	M (masters)
Level 4	Level 6	H (honours)
	Level 5	I (intermediate)
	Level 4	C (certificate)
Level 3		
Level 2		
Level 1		
Entry Level		

In Northern Ireland the Council for the Curriculum, Examinations and Assessment (CCEA) was formed when the Northern Ireland Schools Examinations and Assessment Council (NISEAC) and the Northern Ireland Council for the Curriculum (NICC) merged. CCEA also acts as an independent awarding body, submitting its GCSE and GCE papers to QCA to equate standards.

Vocational qualifications are being developed for each sector by organizations called Sector Skills Councils (SSCs), formerly known as National Training Organizations (NTOs). The SSCs are funded, supported and monitored by the Sector Skills Development Agency (SSDA). The list of Sector Skills Councils can be found on the SSDA website.

As already stated, vocational qualifications are available at a variety of levels; they are competency-based awards which enable the learner to demonstrate that they have the skills and knowledge to undertake a specific set of tasks. These qualifications are based on national occupational standards that have been devised to cover all aspects of specific job roles. The standards include behavioural competencies and underpinning knowledge, as well as referring to the context within which competency must be demonstrated.

Individuals can achieve vocational qualifications within the workplace or via courses provided by colleges and training providers.

Vocational qualifications are offered by a variety of awarding bodies. These are organizations such as City and Guilds, OCR and Edexcel. The qualifications which have been accredited by the QCA are listed on their database which is available at www.openquals.org.uk.

In terms of planning and delivering a programme of development, the occupational standards laid out within the different vocational qualifications provide a useful tool for needs analysis. They enable you to identify gaps in skills and knowledge and to create a programme of activity to fill these gaps.

In vocational training-speak, the person working towards a qualification is termed the candidate and the person who is assessing performance against the competences is the assessor. In order to assess for an NVQ, you must be assessed as occupationally competent in the area that you are delivering and you must hold the relevant Assessor qualification (currently the A1 award).

A good assessor will help a candidate to assess their current position, in terms of their skill and knowledge, help them develop an action plan which will enable them to develop the required competencies and provide ongoing feedback to their candidate on progress. It is the process of planning, implementing action plans, being assessed and receiving feedback that supports the learning of the individual.

In the past, NVQs have been particularly paper-based and have involved producing large portfolios of evidence, not all of it relevant or useful in the day-to-day work of the candidate. However, in recent years the assessment of the qualifications has developed to a point where much of the evidence can be gathered through observation, questioning and 'professional discussion'.

Use it because...

- NVQs are available at a variety of levels and therefore they offer individuals throughout an organization the opportunity to have their skills and knowledge recognized; for some people this can be an excellent motivational tool.
- Vocational qualifications can provide recognition of achievement and an opportunity to reflect upon what could be done better or more effectively. Individuals can achieve recognition for the job that they are currently doing and can see progression routes within that job.
- When an NVQ is being undertaken via an external training provider or at a local college, this provides an opportunity to meet with others from different organizations who are doing a similar job. The advantage here is that there will be the chance to share good practice and learn from other people's experiences.
- These qualifications are very practical and therefore very good for the more pragmatic individuals who wish to see the application of their learning immediately.
- There is some government funding linked to NVQs up to level 2 and therefore this can prove to be cost-effective for the organization.
- It is usually possible to begin these qualifications at any time of the year, especially where they are being delivered in-house.
- Offering recognized qualifications to employees can demonstrate a commitment to staff development that is recognized by customers, employees and external bodies, such as Investors in People.
- These qualifications can be used as part of the organization's quality assurance processes.

Case study: NVQ Level 4 in Management of Learning and Development Provision

Paul Bermingham, Diplomatic Protection Group, Training & Professional Development Unit, Metropolitan Police Service

My current roles and responsibilities are that of Training and Professional Development Manager and Senior Trainer in a high-profile training team within the Police Service. The team is responsible for the training needs analysis (TNA), personal needs analysis, design and delivery of training for over 900 personnel. The training spectrum covers areas of expertise in first aid, personal safety training, coaching and mentoring, legislation, firearms, leadership and management. I have been in the training field for a number of years and have academic and professional qualifications that include: a PGCE, PhD, MA, Member of the Institute of Leadership & Management, Institute of Occupational Learning, College of Teachers, Institute of Quality Assurance, and Chartered Management Institute.

WHY THIS QUALIFICATION?

The reason I chose to undertake this qualification was to broaden my portfolio and to benchmark my activities and future activities against that of a nationally recognized body. To that end my choice of qualification was excellent in its outcome.

The process took some 18 months or so, and in consultation with my NVQ provider I chose the modules relevant to my role. The modules I completed included developing strategies for learning and development, designing learning programmes, managing performance, evaluating and developing my own practice.

Often one struggles to find an appropriate benchmark for the work that one does. In the past, I have relied on comparing good practices within similar teams. In undertaking this qualification, I could work to and develop within a recognized quality assurance framework, in this instance City & Guilds. It also continues to enhance the credibility of what I do both within and outside the service.

OTHER DEVELOPMENTS

Once completed, the units undertaken have been integrated more regularly into daily, as well as long-term, work practices. Quality of training has improved alongside colleagues being able to have a clearer vision of our direction. More senior management have remarked on improvements and a

Training Standards Inspection reported extremely favourably on our practices, processes and structures in place. The quality of all these has arguably been fine-tuned with the implementation of NVQ competencies. Also, the completion of this qualification allowed me to qualify for the City & Guilds Licentiate Award in Management.

Throughout the process, my provider fully supported me with quality feedback, assistance when and where I needed it, in whatever form I needed it (eg face to face, telephone, e-mail etc).

As for the future, this qualification will enable me to open my horizons and opportunities whilst remaining in the training field, especially within management of training. It has also given me the edge, I believe, over my peers in career development and application, alongside improved quality of service and my ability to offer personal development opportunities to my staff.

Making it work

- Because undertaking a vocational qualification takes commitment from the candidate on an ongoing basis, it is important that both the learner and their manager understand why they are participating in the qualification and what outcomes they are expecting once the qualification has been achieved – this provides the motivation and stimulus to continue when the going gets tough.
- Maximize the use of pro formas, computer-based portfolios, witness statements and professional discussion to reduce the amount of paperwork involved.
- The length of time that it takes to build a portfolio can be off-putting and often individuals feel that they are not allocated the appropriate amount of time to prepare their portfolios. In order to build up some momentum, candidates should work with their assessors to plan an assessment strategy that will work for them, eg completing the more straightforward units first or saving these as a 'treat'.
- Individuals participating in NVQs may not feel as if they have learnt anything – this is often due to having a poor assessor. The process of participating in the NVQ should be a reflective one if learning is to be identified – a good assessor will support their candidate in this process.
- Any learner who is participating in an NVQ should have an induction to the programme. The induction will introduce them to the terminology involved, the structure of the qualification and the assessment process.

This is particularly important for those individuals who have no starting knowledge of this type of qualification.

- If offering the qualifications in-house, there must be a range of quality assurance processes in place. Assessors and internal verifiers will need to be found and trained. They will require ongoing support and time will need to be allocated for assessments to be carried out.

It is useful for...

- Competent individuals who need to be encouraged or rewarded for their work.
- Situations where a qualification would be useful for continuing professional development, but where an academic qualification is not appropriate or available.
- Outplacement situations so that employees have an enhancement for their CV.
- Providing evidence of corporate competency.
- Giving individuals a structured programme of development. Progression through the organization can be made dependent upon the achievement of different levels of vocational qualification.
- Supporting departmental and organizational needs analysis. The national occupational standards can help individuals to self-assess and to identify their own learning and development needs. They can also help individuals visualize where their work fits in with their chosen occupation.

References and further reading

The UK National Reference Point for Vocational Qualifications (UK NRP). UK NRP is an independent unit under the management of UK NARIC (see below). UK NRP serves as a first point of contact for national vocational qualifications and is a central information resource for UK skilled worker, trade and technician level qualifications. UK NRP also acts as a national agency representing the UK in a European network of reference points for vocational qualifications in Member States.
Website: www.uknrp.org.uk.

The National Recognition Information Centre for the United Kingdom (UK NARIC). As the national agency responsible for information on international qualifications, the UK NARIC acts as the service provider by providing a recognition and evaluation service of individual awards from overseas and information provision to organizations receiving individuals with international qualifications.

The recognition service and the provision of information are intended to assist and facilitate individual progression towards further studies, professional practice and employment in the UK building on skills and qualifications gained from overseas.
Website: naric.org.uk
The Qualifications and Curriculum Authority (QCA)
Website: www.qca.org.uk
Sector Skills Development Agency (SSDA)
Website: www.ssda.org.uk

REFLECTIVE PRACTICE

In 1984 David Kolb put forward a four-stage learning cycle which is quoted in training and teaching literature alike and which forms the basis of Honey and Mumford's learning styles. Kolb suggested that for learning to happen one must go through the following stages which take the form of a cyclical process:

- Concrete experience: This is a specific experience or event.
- Reflection: The learner considers the experience and thinks about the different aspects that were involved.
- Abstract conceptualization: This is the part of the cycle where the learner creates theories about the experience and draws some general conclusions about what went on.
- Active experimentation: The final part of the cycle will lead back to a further experience or event and it is where the learner puts into practice and applies the new theories that they have created.

See Figure 3.1.

Reflection is considered to be an essential part of the learning process and reflective practice is the method by which reflection is made a conscious and structured activity. Many professions now encourage reflective practice as part of the continuing professional development process; others such as teaching, health and social care regard it as essential to everyday work. (See also Professional Supervision.)

Reflection takes place in many different situations, for example:

- *Incident debriefs*. The emergency services, the armed forces and other organizations that deal with incidents will hold post-incident debriefs where the individuals who have been involved in the incident have the opportunity to consider what happened, how the laid-down procedures were implemented, what worked, what didn't work and what changes to procedures need to be considered. In these high-pressure situations the debrief is also an opportunity to deal with some of the emotions that will have arisen.
- *Project reviews*. A good project manager will hold regular reviews during and at the end of a project. These reviews will involve considering what is going (or went) well, why this is happening (or happened) and what can be done in the future to repeat the positive aspects. There will also be consideration of the difficulties/challenges, why these are arising (or arose) and how they can be prevented in the future.
- *Critical incident analysis*. In this situation the incident is simply an event that stood out for the learner. This could be a particularly positive or particularly negative experience, eg a sales executive gaining a very large order or a customer service adviser dealing with a particularly irate client. The reflection in this case involves considering what the situation was, when and where it took place and why it was particularly memorable. The learner then goes on to consider what their part in the situation was, how they interpret their own and others' behaviour, the impact of their actions and the actions of others and what their major learning points could be from the way in which they dealt with the situation.
- *Self-talk*. Most people will have conversations with themselves at the end of a day, some out loud, some in their heads. This does not suggest that most people have a mental illness, but is simply a way of processing what has gone on during the day. This process of analysing what was said and done in different situations is a natural learning process which can be capitalized upon by maintaining a reflective journal.

Reflective journals

A reflective journal is a record of learning that has taken place as a result of reflecting on experiences and situations. A journal should be a personal document and it does not even need to be in the form of a paper-based or electronic document, it could be in the form of tape recordings. Some useful questions to consider when making entries into a journal would be:

- What happened today? Which particular situations or experiences stand out in my mind?
- What was my role in this situation? What did I do or say? What didn't I do or say?
- Why did I behave as I did in the situation?
- What did others do or say?
- What impact did my behaviour have on others and their behaviour on me?
- How might a fly-on-the-wall view this situation?
- If I was in this situation again, what would I do differently? What would I do the same?
- What are the main learning points that I can gain from this situation?
- How do these learning points relate to previous situations and my learning from them?
- How will these learning points impact on my actions in the future?
- How am I developing?

Use it because...

- True learning cannot take place without reflection.
- Reflection and review of situations and experiences provides the learner and the organization with the opportunity to make sense of situations, to view them from different angles and, in some cases, to reframe them, ie to put them into a different, usually more positive, context. Reflection gives learners the chance to 'hold a mirror' up to their experiences and to potentially see themselves as others see them.
- Reflection has benefits for all levels of an organization. Organizations should attempt to encourage and reward reflection, rather than frowning on individuals who are seen to be 'sitting and staring into space'.
- Reflection promotes double loop learning by providing the opportunity to consider not just the 'how' but 'why' things are done.

Making it work

To be most effective, reflective practice needs to include the following three elements:

1 thinking about what you are doing whilst you are doing it (reflection-in-action);

2 thinking about what you have done after you have done it (reflection-on-action);
3 working with a mentor, coach or supervisor who will ask appropriate and probing questions to encourage reflection and to ensure that the reflection does not simply become a 'navel-gazing' process.

Reflection-in-action and reflection-on-action were activities discussed in *The Reflective Practitioner* by Donald Schön (1983).

Other techniques to make it successful are:

- *Building reflection into everyday activities.* Give individuals a reflective journal and/or have a reflection activity as a standing agenda item for team meetings. Encourage the use of 'dead' or downtime such as travel time or gaps in production.
- *Responding to different learning styles.* Reflection takes time and it does not come naturally to everyone. As Honey and Mumford have demonstrated with their learning-styles questionnaire, many individuals will have a preference for activity-based learning and to spend time on reflection will feel very uncomfortable for them. By involving activists in the process of reflection, for example by asking them to facilitate group reflection or to verbalize their reflections, they will be more inclined to participate. Equally, a pragmatist will want to reflect on how to apply their learning and a theorist will want to understand all the theories before they are willing to reflect – to respond to these learning styles, encourage the individuals to reflect around either the application of the learning or the underpinning theories.
- *Recognizing reflection time as productive time.* Set up quiet areas within the workplace. If your organization uses time sheets or monitors time usage, include a code or section for reflective practice.

It is useful for...

- Creating a learning culture within a team or organization.
- Reflection should be built into every activity, project or piece of work in order to maximize learning from everyday activity.
- Systematic reflective practice is beneficial for more competent and skilled individuals whose focus is on enhancement of skills, knowledge and attitudes rather than learning techniques and behaviours.
- Meeting CPD requirements.

References and further reading

Atherton, J S (2005a) *Learning and Teaching: Critical reflection* [Online], UK: Available: http://www.learningandteaching.info/learning/critical1.htm

Atherton, J S (2005b) *Learning and Teaching: Reflection and reflective practice* [Online], UK: Available: http://www.learningandteaching.info/learning/reflecti.htm

Schön, D A (1983) *The Reflective Practitioner: How professionals think in action*, Temple Smith, London

Smith, M K (2001) Donald Schön: learning, reflection and change, in *the encyclopedia of informal education*, www.infed.org/thinkers/et-schon.htm

SECONDMENTS

Secondments refer to the temporary transfer of a member of staff to either another department or team within an organization, or to a different organization altogether. In the latter case, this might be another company, a government department or a charity. Fundamentally, someone is temporarily given a different role or job for a fixed period of time. This may be to take on a specific project, to cover a vacant position or sometimes because the work of their current role has decreased or is not required and the organization does not wish to lose the person via redundancy as they will be required in the future. Larger organizations are increasingly seeing secondments to charities or community groups as a method for achieving their corporate responsibility goals.

There is no fixed length to secondments although they most commonly last between 3 and 12 months; this may be decided on by the learning goals of the individual, the need of the accepting department or organization, or company policy. The question of who pays depends on the purpose of the secondment – companies will have their own policies and, in our experience, it usually boils down to negotiation between budget managers! A short secondment or one that primarily benefits the individual is often paid by the 'lending' department. A longer secondment may be funded from project costs or existing manpower budgets. Often companies lending personnel to charities and not-for-profit organizations will continue to pay all or part of the person's salary.

Internally, secondment opportunities arise most commonly from recruitment needs, and therefore can be initiated by the HR department, a manager or an individual. Sometimes they can be suggested by an individual or a manager in response to a development review – 'I need X to learn more about budgets, can they come and work in your area during the budget-setting process?'

External opportunities can be initiated by an organization either asking for or offering to give assistance. In 1982, Business in the Community was founded to assist companies meet their community responsibilities; its purpose is to 'inspire, challenge, engage and support business in continually improving its positive impact on society'. Other organizations that coordinate secondment opportunities are: Employees in the Community Network, Interchange, and The Whitehall and Industry Group.

Use it because...

- It provides staff development opportunities which may not be available within the department or organization, such as managing staff or working on a project.
- Secondments are an excellent way of staffing short-term projects or activities, especially fulfilling short-term expertise and knowledge requirements. For example, a customer services department wishing to review its procedures may require a full-time business analyst for the first three months of the project and a full-time trainer for the next three. Seconding these specialists allows such flexibility.
- The secondee gains a wider experience and acquires new skills, whilst maintaining the stability of knowing they can return to their permanent role.
- The learner is able to practise and apply their skills in a different setting from the one within which they normally work.
- The employer and/or manager not only gains from the individual's development, but also gains from improved cross-functional relationships and communication.
- Secondments improve morale and motivation by demonstrating an organization's commitment to development. Also, 'a change is as good as a rest' and the secondee returns to their permanent position refreshed and reinvigorated.
- Companies providing secondments to public organizations and charities are seen to be good contributors to the community and good employers, which helps with recruitment and retention because employees' altruistic needs are met.
- The receiving department or organization gains assistance with projects, the opportunity to develop their own staff via skills transfer and also an external perspective on their work processes and procedures.

Making it work

1. Be clear on the purpose(s) of the secondment – why are you doing it and what will be gained by the lending organization/department, the receiving team, the individual? Establish clear outcomes and objectives, which are agreed with all parties.
2. Use local and national networks to establish external opportunities.
3. Make the recruitment process for secondments fair and open. If it is not a true selection process, then please don't pretend it is. If you ask for applicants, then follow recruitment best practice – you will only have to deal with dissatisfied staff who were not selected, and it is easier to do this if the terms of selection are clear in the first place.
4. Advertise your secondment policy across the organization, ideally in writing.
5. Plan the secondment with sufficient time for the secondee to train another member of the team to undertake their work, prior to the secondment happening, so that the team or department is not disadvantaged by skill or staffing shortages.
6. Make sure that communication channels with secondees are continued – they will need to be informed, and where appropriate, consulted about changes and developments in their lending department, especially if they are in another organization. It is not a case that they can be forgotten until they return, or as one manager we know did, decide that there was not a job for them to return to and failed to mention it to anyone until the week before the person was due to return!
7. Monitor secondments throughout: Are objectives being achieved? Is the secondee happy? Is it working? Do they have the support they need? The secondee may find it difficult to adjust or fit into the new team or department culture and will appreciate ongoing support.
8. Review at the end: What experiences has the learner had? What learning has occurred? How will that affect their performance/behaviour in the future? What's next for their development?
9. Plan the secondee's return – the individual can find it difficult to return to their original role, especially if the secondment was in an organization or department that is very different to their own.
10. Advertise successful secondments so that others know it works!

It is useful for...

- Filling a vacancy in a team or project; the learner can usefully apply their skills and knowledge, as well as gain from the experience – either by working in a new area or with different people.

- Learners who have good technical skills and need to enhance their communication, interpersonal, team-working or project skills.
- Individuals who are good technically but need the challenge of doing the work in a different environment or culture. For example, an HR manager who knows their subject and would benefit from experience in a unionized organization.
- Extending technical or specialist skills, by working with other specialists.
- Trying out roles to see if they suit the person, their skills and knowledge. It is a good way of giving someone experience that is relevant to their next career move, such as promotion to a line management role.

Reference and further reading

Jackson, T (2006) 'Career Development', CIPD factsheet, CIPD, London

SELF-STUDY

We are using the term 'self-study' to cover informal activities which involve learning through seeking information or being provided with information for a specific purpose. It is learning which is self-directed and takes place via one or more of the following methods:

- reading;
- internet;
- audio cassettes or CDs;
- video;
- TV/radio;
- reflection and critical incident analysis (see also separate section on Reflective Practice);
- observation.

When undertaking self-study, the learner takes responsibility for their own learning and for the methods that they choose to use. The learner will set their own objectives (which may be very specific or very broad) and will self-assess to decide whether they have fulfilled their objectives.

Self-study can be very effective and have a profound impact upon the learner because the information that they are learning is not filtered by an external body; however, it can mean that the learner could become diverted along the 'wrong' track, ie one that is not relevant or accurate.

Self-study is often prompted by a specific need, for example being asked to make a presentation. In this situation, the learner knows that they will be put under the 'spotlight' and therefore they are likely to be highly motivated to seek correct and applicable information. Making a presentation is an excellent way to check understanding of a topic – if you can explain it to others you generally understand what you are explaining.

Use it because...

- Self-study can be cost- and time-effective.
- It is flexible. Individuals can learn what they need, when they need it and at a time and place of their choosing.
- Self-study encourages self-development and self-reliance; it can help individuals learn to learn and to value their own resources.
- Learners will be highly motivated because they know why they are studying and what they need to learn.

Making it work

Give the learner the checklist shown below.

Tips for self-study

- Set yourself specific learning objectives which begin with the phrase 'when I have completed this learning I will be able to...'
- Rephrase your objectives into a series of questions which will help you to filter the information that you are gathering.
- Access a variety of sources of information and, if possible, check on their validity, currency and context.
- Where possible, discuss what you have learnt with others in order to help process and apply the information.
- Keep a list of sources of information and notes to assist in the reflective process.
- Assess your learning against your objectives. Ask yourself, 'how do I know that I have achieved this learning objective?'
- Consider how you will apply the knowledge to your current or future situation. How can this period of learning benefit you and/or your organization?

- Agree deadlines and allocate time for self-study. Follow up with the learner to ensure that they are achieving their objectives. This method is very reliant on the individual and people with busy lives may find that they are easily distracted and do not stick to their self-imposed deadlines.
- The learner may find it difficult to set themselves specific objectives and may need your help to do this.
- If there are important facts that need to be covered, bring these to the attention of the learner at the start of the process so that they can ensure they find the necessary information. This also serves to give them a starting point for their explorations.
- Provide the individuals with a list of available resources and information about where they can be found.
- Evaluate at an agreed point to see if learning objectives have been met, because the learner may either have stopped studying or be on a constant mission for more information.
- Consider having a dedicated resource centre that learners can use whenever they wish. Include in the resource centre organization documents such as project reviews, written procedures and, if appropriate, case notes.

It is useful for...

- Studying an academic or conceptual subject.
- Highly theoretical or academic learners.
- Individuals who cannot be released from their 'day job'.
- Filling a gap when there are no structured learning opportunities available.
- Solving a current problem where the learner needs an answer right away or does not know how to do a specific task.
- Individuals preparing for promotion, job change or a change in career direction.
- Learners who want to keep abreast of changes in their field.
- New teams that are about to undertake a project where they feel that they have limited knowledge of the subject matter.
- Situations where someone asks the learner a question and they do not currently have the answer, but promise to get back to the questioner.

SHADOWING

Job shadowing involves the learner spending time observing someone else who is carrying out a job. They spend time watching, listening and learning what the job is about and what is involved in a typical day's work, without actually carrying out the job itself.

In addition to the developmental benefits, job shadowing is also an excellent networking tool, helping to improve communication across departments, and providing opportunities for sharing best practice.

Job shadowing can take place for an hour, over a day, or for longer depending on the nature of the job and the learning objectives to be achieved.

The City University London job shadowing scheme, as detailed on their website, offers three models for shadowing:

1. *Fly on the wall* – where the person being shadowed just gets on with their work as if the shadower is not present. The shadower makes notes and little, if any, discussion about the work occurs. Third parties are told who the person is but are asked to pretend that they are not there. This means that the person who is being shadowed is allowed to continue with no disruption to their work, but the lack of interaction means that learning is limited.
2. *Burst interaction* – this is similar to the fly-on-the-wall model, except that the person being shadowed briefs the shadower about the next piece of work or activity coming up and discusses what happened after they have carried it out. During the activity, the shadower maintains a fly-on-the-wall role and does not interact with the task. At the end of the day, a fuller review and reflection is carried out. This approach allows for items to be discussed during the day, but without interruption to the actual work itself. It allows the shadower to ask questions and seek greater understanding. However, it is more time-consuming and productivity for the day will be reduced.
3. *Continuous interaction* – the shadower is involved in the work process. The person being shadowed can explain what they are doing as they do it, and if appropriate, the shadower can ask questions at the time they occur. This provides a high level of interaction and discussion which maximizes learning but does slow down the work.

Adapted from www.city.ac.uk/sd/job/index.html

Use it because...

- It allows the learner to have room to consider the skill or role and explore it without being tied into actually having to do it.
- The learner doesn't actually do the work and therefore they do not make any on-the-job mistakes.
- Learning is via observation and therefore the job still gets done, albeit on some occasions more slowly.
- It provides the opportunity to ask questions there and then, which means that learning, as well as being timely and relevant to the task, focuses on what the learner needs to know.
- It is real, and therefore you do not have to set up simulations or expensive exercises; it allows the learner to apply their previous knowledge and experiences to true situations.
- It promotes team and cross-functional working which improves relationships as two people are required to work closely together. This results in greater understanding of other people's roles, what they do and where they fit into the bigger picture.
- It can support the development of a learning organization by involving a range of staff, and not just the 'training department'. It shows that learning can be achieved through observation and reflection on every-day activity.

Making it work

The key to successful learning via job shadowing is preparation. This reduces the opportunity for anyone involved to view it as a 'jolly'. Prior to any shadowing experience, work with the learner to answer the following questions:

- What do you want to get out of the experience? Set your objectives.
- Are there any specific aspects of the role you are interested in seeing or finding out about? How will you ensure that you will find out about them?
- What particular questions do you want to find answers to?
- How involved do you want to be? How involved should you be given the type of work? What are the health and safety implications? Do you need additional equipment?
- What do others need to be told? Do you need their permission to be present? What confidentiality issues might arise?

- How will you use your learning?
- How does this fit into your overall development plan?
- What are the benefits for the person being shadowed?

Once the learner has answered these questions, they should arrange a meeting with the person that they will be shadowing to discuss their objectives and make practical arrangements for the experience. The person who is being shadowed may artificially arrange their day or activity. This may be useful to ensure that the learner is getting what they need from the shadowing. Equally, it may not be desirable as it may give a false (often rosy) picture of the role – this often happens when a manager goes to shadow staff as part of their induction.

As the sponsor of the learning event, you may want to discuss the purpose and process yourself with the person being shadowed. This will ensure that the person who is being shadowed is fully committed and that they don't feel that this is management's way of watching them, or that they have been loaded with additional work.

It is important that the learner pays attention during the shadowing. Because it is not a participative process, it can be quite easy to drift off and miss something. The key to making this work is to ensure that the learner uses their observation skills – you may want to explore with the learner what these skills are and how to use them prior to the event.

In order to maximize their learning, the shadower must reflect on and review their experience as soon as possible after the event – questions for them to ask themselves are:

- What did you learn about the job, the skills and knowledge used?
- How can you use this learning and what does it mean to you?
- How will you change what you do and how you do it as a result of this experience?
- What else do you need to know or learn about this job, task or role?

It is useful for...

- Giving people an awareness and understanding of what other jobs involve and what other people do. It is therefore excellent for company induction, especially giving a wider understanding of the business to specialist, support or senior staff.
- Career development – helping people to understand their options and therefore make informed decisions about their next job move.

- The beginning or middle stages of a development plan, not at the end. Used at the beginning it can help clarify what specific skills the learner needs to develop in addition to the ones they already have. Used in the middle, it can help to transfer learning from a training course – shadowing someone who uses the skill that the learner has recently been trained in will help them see it being put into practice and provide useful insights into its real-life application. Given the purpose of shadowing is to gain understanding about a role or task, using shadowing at the end of a development plan may be a little late, as one assumes that by the end of the plan, the learner has developed the necessary skills and knowledge to carry out the job.
- Reflectors and pragmatists, but not so good for activists, who will want to be more involved in doing the job itself.

Reference and further reading

Paris, K and Mason, S (1995) *Planning and Implementing Youth Apprenticeship and Work-based Learning*, University of Wisconsin, Center on Education and Work, Madison, WI

TEMPORARY PROMOTION

Temporary promotion is used throughout a range of organizations, especially within the public sector, to provide development opportunities for individuals, but mainly to fulfil a business need when a vacancy arises. This strategy may also be used when a peak in work levels requires additional support at a higher level. Temporary promotion involves an individual 'acting up' or taking on, for a specified period of time, a position that is one level above them in the organizational structure, eg a deputy manager taking on the role of manager.

Use it because...

- It provides opportunities for individuals to develop skills whilst fulfilling a business need.
- It demonstrates a commitment to staff development as it shows that the organization actively seeks to offer opportunities for staff to learn by doing.

- The organization has the chance to see how individuals perform at higher levels and whether permanent promotion should be considered. Additionally, it actively demonstrates a policy of internal promotion.
- Vacancies can be filled more quickly, thereby ensuring continuity of work.
- Individuals have the chance to try out a role for a fixed period, to gain experience which can enhance their CV and career options.

Making it work

1. Define the period of the temporary promotion. Factors to consider include how long it will take to recruit for the position, how long it will take the member of staff who is temporarily promoted to fully understand the role and become effective in the role and whether it will be possible to backfill the position which is made vacant by the temporary promotion.
2. Review the job description and person specification for the position that has become vacant. These may need to be amended before filling the vacancy.
3. Decide upon the method in which the vacancy will be advertised. Will the position be advertised throughout the organization or will advertising be restricted to the department where the vacancy exists? Will you advertise the position, or do you already know who you will temporarily promote? How does this fit in with your equal opportunities and recruitment policies? The recruitment procedures that you use to select the individual for temporary promotion should be the same procedures as would be used for filling any vacancy to ensure equality of opportunity and objectivity of the final appointment.
4. In order to maximize the development opportunity, consider rotating the temporary promotion between several people so that as many staff as possible benefit.
5. Clarify the learning needs of the individual who will be temporarily promoted; agree clear objectives and methods to meet the needs within the time available.
6. Plan the experience so that benefits exist for both the individual and the organization. This will include setting specific objectives for the individual who is temporarily promoted that are realistic and can be achieved within the timescales of the promotion. You will also require processes to monitor progress during the period of the promotion and an agreed evaluation process, which could be your organization's performance appraisal system.

Issues to be aware of when you are planning a temporary promotion are:

- Temporary promotion can raise the expectations of the individuals who are temporarily promoted and when they return to their permanent role they may find the transition 'downwards' difficult. Address this by, if possible, agreeing beforehand a return strategy and include this subject in your evaluation meeting.
- Temporary promotion can cause problems for the department which loses the individual who has been temporarily promoted because their work will still need to be completed. Perhaps this is an opportunity to give somebody else temporary promotion or additional responsibility.
- The individual who is temporarily promoted may not be able to gain full support and respect from team members when they know that the promotion will be for a fixed period. A conversation about how the individual will gain this respect could be part of the pre-promotion meeting. Non-cooperation by team members should be addressed initially informally and then, if it continues, escalated through your disciplinary processes.

It is useful for...

- An individual who requires experience to complement the skills and knowledge that they have in order to get their next job.
- Organizations where the career development model is well defined and includes temporary promotion within it.
- Situations where a real business need exists and where time is of the essence.
- Activists and pragmatists who will benefit from the opportunity to learn by doing the job.

TRADE EXHIBITIONS

Trade exhibitions bring together organizations which have an interest in specific fields, for example IT exhibitions, business exhibitions and so on. At first glance these events may not immediately be seen as development opportunities; however, they provide individuals with the chance to:

- assess new products and services that are relevant to their particular field;
- network with other individuals from their area of interest;

- consider different options that may be available to them in dealing with specific situations.

Use it because...

- Trade exhibitions bring together a wide range of suppliers, current topics and issues under one roof, therefore you can access a variety of information sources easily.
- They provide time away from the workplace to reflect upon what is happening on a day-to-day basis and consider the future.
- They raise awareness of the current trends and developments within a particular field.
- They can refocus or reawaken curiosity and passion for an area of interest.
- Trade exhibitions are often without cost.

Making it work

- Choose the exhibition carefully to ensure that it offers something new and different for the learner that they will be able to use.
- At a large exhibition it may not be possible to visit all the stands in one day or to find the ones that will be useful; if possible, obtain a list from the exhibition organizer and plan the visit. Some exhibitions will allow you to pre-book appointments with different exhibitors via their website.
- Have clear outcomes to be achieved; this will prevent visits to exhibitions being seen as a 'jolly' rather than a day's work.
- Dedicate time for identifying what has been gained by attending the exhibition and how the learning will be used.

It is useful for...

- This method can be used to broaden a learner's thinking around the options available to them for a specific piece of work. It can also give an insight into different career options that might be available within a specific field.
- Visiting an exhibition can often be a useful way to re-energize and re-motivate an individual who has been doing a certain job for a length of time. An individual who is feeling that they have reached a dead end

or does not know what their next step might be may find this method useful for them as it can identify different options.

- A trade exhibition can provide opportunities for personal development in the area of getting to know others, introducing yourself to strangers and increasing confidence in new environments. It can be the first step to participating in more formal networking events.
- Consider letting the learner work on a stand or present at a trade exhibition as a way of developing organizing, interpersonal and/or presenting skills.
- Finally, an individual who wishes to raise their profile and access different networks will find this method helpful.

TRAINING COURSES

Sloman, writing for the CIPD (2005), defines training as 'an instructor-led and content-based intervention leading to desired changes in behaviour'.

A training course brings together a group of individuals to learn specific skills, knowledge and behaviours as defined by the stated aims and objectives of the course. Training courses can be run within an organization or external to an organization, by in-house trainers or external trainers.

Training courses have traditionally been the way that most learning has been delivered within organizations. There are a number of reasons for this, including:

- A course can be planned and delivered within a reasonably short timescale.
- Sending an employee on a training course is a visible and tangible intervention.
- Training courses may seem to mirror the type of learning that most people have experienced before entering the workplace, ie school, college and university.
- Managers see training courses as a way to provide development for their staff with minimum input from themselves – in many organizations managers perceive that it is the role of the training or HR department to source training for their staff.
- There is a wide range of courses available and many organizations find this menu of options very appealing – for some, it is appealing because it prevents them having to think too hard about what development is needed and how to provide it. For others, the list covers most of the subjects they are likely to want and provides a ready-made development plan.

Use it because...

- *A training course provides the opportunity to cover a wide range of material within a relatively short time period.* Using a variety of training techniques, including accelerated learning techniques, it is possible to cover a large amount of information within a short space of time during a training course. The use of exercises to reinforce and contextualize the learning can help participants to relate the knowledge to their own situation.
- *Training courses can be used to target large numbers of learners.* Some training courses will accommodate up to a hundred learners and even when delivering a course to smaller groups, it is possible to repeat the course so that large numbers can be trained and the same aims and objectives can be covered for all groups.

  A variety of methods that will appeal to a wide range of learners can be used.

  Training courses can include presentations, group work, case studies, role plays and individual reflection, as well as a wide range of exercises. A well-designed course will utilize several of these methods appealing to the range of learning styles within the group, enabling learners to maximize their learning.

  Courses provide the opportunity to exchange ideas with others – networking, learning from other people and sharing best practice.

  One of the most important elements of a training course for many individuals is the opportunity to meet others who share the same interests and, often, the same issues as they do. Whether the course is external or in-house, the different environment can encourage participants to share with each other and to learn from each other. Lunchtimes and break times during day-courses and the evening sessions in the bar for residential courses can provide as much learning as the formal sessions.

  Courses, particularly those delivered in-house, can be tailored to meet the specific needs that have been identified within the organization.

  When an organization discovers that a group of people have the same training need, a course which has been designed with these needs in mind can be an effective and efficient means of addressing these needs.
- *Training can be delivered when it is convenient for the organization.* For many organizations, it can be easier to plan time out for individuals to attend training courses than it is to plan time for on-job training or other types of learning. Many managers feel more comfortable if their staff are away from their workplace attending a course than they do if

the member of staff is at their workstation reading or engaging in an online learning session.

- *Courses can provide individuals with the opportunity to step back from their day-to-day work and to reflect upon what is currently happening.* Sometimes, attending a training course might be the only time that an individual has to take time to reflect and have an objective view on what is happening in their workplace. This time to reflect can be invaluable.

  For some individuals, being allowed to attend a training course can make them feel valued. Individuals view reward and recognition in very different ways. Some individuals will feel that they are valued and that their contribution is recognized if their employer is willing to invest time and money in sending them on a training course. The 'value-added' elements of increased motivation and willingness to try something new and creative can sometimes outweigh the costs of an external training course.
- *Training courses can be used very effectively to raise awareness of certain issues that are current within an organization.* If there are legislative issues affecting an organization or there is a change in policy, procedure or systems, running a training programme to raise awareness can be the most effective way of disseminating information to all staff within as short a space of time as possible.

Making it work

The following are the elements of an effective training course:

- The course must have an overall aim and a set of specific, achievable and measurable objectives, which are ideally signed off by the course sponsor.
- The course objectives must be in line with the identified training need(s).
- The trainer who will deliver the course should be fully briefed about the required content and the issues that they are likely to face from participants attending the course. Issues that trainers need to be aware of include participants' reluctance to attend, issues about the subject or events happening back in their workplace, such as major change or restructuring.
- The trainer or training company should be selected according to their responsiveness to your needs, knowledge of the subject and fit with your organization culture. It is advisable to take up references and also meet the trainer in advance.

- The participant must see the relevance of what they will get from the course. This can be achieved by line managers conducting pre-course briefings and ensuring that courses meet current and identified needs. See the Time Management case study in Chapter 6, see page 147.
- The training methods that are used to deliver the course must be relevant to the subject matter and must appeal to the range of learning styles within the group. Methods should not be chosen because the trainer likes them or because they are the latest trend.
- The course should cover the four areas of Kolb's learning cycle – an activity, reflection on the activity, input and/or development of theories and application to real-life situations.
- The course must provide the opportunity for participants to learn some theory and/or practical skills and to consider how this can be applied to their work. The course will be most effective where the participants have an opportunity to practise their skills within the training setting and to receive some feedback from the trainer.
- There should be some way of assessing participants' learning, whether this is by a test at the start and end of the course or by a simple self-analysis.
- A method of evaluating participants' reactions to the course, the environment and the trainer needs to be included.
- There should be a method of evaluating how participants have implemented their learning in the workplace. For courses to be successful participants need to be able to implement their learning, with support as required, as soon after the course as possible. Evaluation of this may take place some weeks after the course.

There are a number of drawbacks to training courses. These are:

- *Cost.* Training courses, especially external courses, can be expensive – from £100 per person per day to £1,500+, depending on the nature of the course. The cost of the course may not be the only funding that must be found; money may need to be allocated to pay for cover for the person who is attending the course, plus travel and subsistence costs and the cost of any lost business due to the absence of the course participant. Please note that in our experience, there is not necessarily a correlation between cost and quality!
- *Learning can be difficult to measure.* Unless a thorough pre-course assessment is carried out as well as a post-course assessment, the amount of learning that has taken place may be difficult to quantify. This may be especially apparent for training courses relating to 'soft'

skills and for some management development programmes. Managers and participants often 'forget' or are unwilling to evaluate training after the event.

- *Training courses can be too general and may not address individual learning needs.* Because training courses are aimed at groups of individuals, it may not be possible to address each individual need within the group or to pitch the material at just the right level for each individual. It is often up to the participant to ensure that they have achieved their personal objectives for the training course.
- *The effectiveness of the course depends on the skills of the trainer.* As in all walks of life, there are some excellent trainers, some average trainers and some trainers who should not be allowed to call themselves trainers! Simply having a training qualification does not guarantee that the individual will be an effective trainer. Equally, teachers do not always make good trainers of adults (even those teachers who have been trained in post-16 education), as teaching tends to be about showing or telling as opposed to assisting learners to discover something for themselves (ITOL, *A Glossary of UK Training And Occupational Learning Terms*). If an organization is seeking someone who has good training skills, it is recommended that they see the person in action and refer to feedback from others who have experienced this person's training.
- *Learners need to apply their learning straightaway in order to embed it.* Often, individuals are sent on training courses in preparation for a future task. In order for learning to be embedded and reinforced, it is important that the learner has the opportunity to put their new skills into practice as soon as possible following the training event. This is important for all types of training, from communication skills training to software training. The old adage 'use it or lose it' applies in this situation.
- *Effective training requires an appropriate space.* If training is to be effective, it is important that it is delivered within an environment that is conducive to learning. This means that there should be sufficient space for a variety of training activities and that appropriate training aids should be available. As well as sufficient space, the learning environment needs a positive, relaxed and safe ambiance. In order to meet Maslow's lower-level human needs, participants should have access to food, water and toilet facilities.
- *Need to provide cover when people are away from their desks.* For some organizations, particularly small or medium-sized ones or organizations that employ a range of specialists, it may not be possible to release individuals to attend training courses. Even in organizations where there

are a number of individuals doing the same job, the cost of providing cover may be prohibitive. Training courses usually take place during traditional office hours, which can be a problem for shift workers.

- *Objectives may not actually meet needs.* A training course may be identified to meet individual needs; however, having attended the course it is sometimes possible to find that the objectives do not quite address the specific issues that the individual needed to cover.
- *Organizing courses takes time.* Whilst training courses can be set up at reasonably short notice, organizing an effective training event requires attention to a range of issues and details. For a course to be truly effective, it will require pre-course, during the course and post-course support and administration, which can be time consuming.
- *Participants sometimes do not want to attend.* Because some managers do not brief their staff about the training courses that they are going to attend and do not agree the objectives with them, some participants may not be clear about why they are on the course and what they want to get from it. This can mean that time is taken during the course identifying these issues rather than working towards the course objectives. Sometimes participants have not been given feedback and therefore do not accept that they have a learning need. They therefore approach the course with a negative attitude and/or the comment 'I'm here because I was sent'.

  Residential courses can be useful; however, many participants may have commitments that would make it difficult for them to be away from home. If there is no need for them to be there between the end of one day and the start of the next, then provide accommodation as an option, rather than a requirement. If there is evening work, tell them what is expected and let them make their choice about whether to stay after the work is completed or to travel home. If a residential course is essential, give people plenty of notice so that they can make the appropriate domestic arrangements, and do not make changes unless absolutely necessary.
- *The course is trainer-focused rather than learner-focused.* In some cases, usually where the trainer is not experienced, the focus can be on the trainer rather than the learner, which means that it is unlikely that the learners' objectives will be met. On some occasions, the trainer tries to include everything that they know on a subject, rather than what should be covered in order to meet the learners' needs or organization's requirements.
- *No follow-up from manager.* Without follow-up after the course from the individual's manager, it is likely that the learning that took place

will not be implemented in the workplace. In order for changes in behaviour to take place, it is important that these changes be identified and supported.

- *It is difficult to measure the return on investment.* Some managers will not take the time or have the skills to measure the return on investment for training courses. It can be difficult to place a value on the outcomes of courses objectively, making it difficult to assess benefit against cost. Because training courses can be costly to implement, it is important to decide what return is being sought and how its achievement will be measured.
- *Training courses are often planned in isolation with no idea of how success will be evaluated.* Where training courses are run as a 'knee-jerk' reaction to a certain problem or situation, time is sometimes not taken to really consider the outcomes that are required. If training courses are to be effective, managers must decide what they will be looking for after the training course that is different from what was happening before the course. They must define the required outcomes and take the time to measure whether or not they have been achieved.
- *Quantity rather than quality.* Some organizations have targets for the number of training hours per employee. Whilst these targets ensure that some training takes place, they do not ensure that the quality of learning is high or that needs have been met.

It is useful for...

- Delivering a consistent message to large numbers of people.
- Developing individuals with each of the different learning styles.
- Factual, knowledge and skill-based learning, eg software packages, first aid, health and safety.
- Updating organizations on changes to legislation, procedures and systems.
- Learning techniques and processes, eg negotiation, interviewing, assertiveness – skills which are later developed through practice.

References and further reading

There are many excellent books and resources available to trainers. The list includes:

Rae, L (2001) *Develop your Training Skills*, Kogan Page, London

Rae, L (2002) *Trainer Assessment: A guide to measuring the performance of trainers and facilitators*, Gower, Aldershot
Rea, D G (1994) *Selecting Training Methods*, Kogan Page, London
Sloman, M (2005) *Training to Learning. Change agenda*, CIPD, London
Thorpe, S and Clifford, J (2000) *Dear Trainer: Dealing with difficult problems in training*, Kogan Page, London

ORGANIZATIONAL LEARNING METHODS

In Chapter 3, we discussed the importance of organizational learning and how individual learning must be used to develop the way organizations work, their practices and processes. Any development method will assist with organizational learning if followed up properly; however, the following methods specifically encourage the sharing of information and skills:

- Action learning
- Coaching
- Delegation
- Discussion groups and boards
- Job shadowing
- Mentoring
- Networking
- On-the-job training
- Professional membership
- Projects
- Secondments.

Other ideas for promoting organizational learning are:

- Develop a knowledge management system – either a library or intranet site for documents and information that others may find useful, such as project plans, review sheets, technical papers, manuals, reports.
- Create a learning centre – where staff can research information, use e-learning packages, access written material etc.
- Establish an intranet chat room or discussion group.
- Ensure that carrying out reviews forms a regular part of your processes, so that it becomes a normal practice for teams, project groups as well as individuals. We are still amazed by how many people fail to ask at least 'what went well?', 'what didn't go well?' about a piece of work before starting their next major task! Expect that summaries of these reviews

are circulated, so that you know that they happen, and so the learning from them is spread as far as possible.

- Regularly review processes and working methods – ask why you are doing something, as well as how can you do it better.
- Ask participants who attend training courses, networking events, conferences etc to share their experience via a short presentation to their colleagues. This will consolidate their learning and reduce the amount of money that you spend on sending lots of people to the same event, as well as promote the communication of information.
- Publicize who has undertaken what development so that others know who has what knowledge, skills and competence.
- Communicate plans for change widely and as far ahead as is practical. Encourage staff to offer ideas and suggestions about the plans, as there may be something that has been overlooked that is essential to the organization.

5

Selecting the Right Methods

With such a wide range of different development methods available to you, which one do you choose to successfully meet the learning needs of the individual and the organization? There are no definite rules about which method is suitable for any given situation. However, in this chapter we have provided a checklist of questions that can be used to help you select the most appropriate method(s), followed by some information about each area for consideration. Working through this checklist, whilst considering the different methods available to you, will help you to construct development plans which work for you and your learners. We talk more about development plans in Chapter 6.

CHECKLIST FOR SELECTING DEVELOPMENT METHODS

In order to select the most appropriate method the following questions will need to be answered:

1 What are the required outcomes?
2 Who has this development need?
3 What is the deadline?
4 What are the organizational factors that need to be considered?
5 What budget is available?
6 What resources are available?

Clarifying the required outcomes

Outcomes are defined as the results that will be achieved when the learning needs are met and as such is a tangible (preferably in writing) statement of what the learner will know or be able to do differently at the end of the learning experience. The outcomes are created from the learning needs analysis, and therefore you will want to know what the needs are and how they were identified. Depending upon your involvement with the needs analysis, you may want to validate that the real need has been recognized by reviewing the qualitative and quantitative data, seeing how it links to the business vision and plans and understanding the consequences of not addressing it. This will act as a check to ensure that it is truly a developmental need and not a performance or procedural issue.

Focus your outcomes on what additional knowledge or skill the learner will have when this need has been addressed and what they will do differently as a result of the development – what different results will the learner produce? What will you see or hear that is different?

Think about how you will measure the achievement and success as this may directly link to the method that should be used, eg if you are going to measure the level of their learning by on-job assessment, the appropriate method will allow them to practise the job prior to the assessment and then demonstrate their competence during the assessment.

It is at this stage that the aims and objectives are written, detailing the milestones that will need to be achieved in order to reach the final outcome. This may result in a different method being selected for each of the objectives. It is rare that one method is able to offer all the learning that is required by the learner – this relates back to what we have said about training courses and how their effect is minimized when they 'stand alone'. The next chapter gives some examples of how a variety of methods can be incorporated into a development plan.

In an ideal world, the outcomes that are finally agreed will be signed off by both the learner(s) and the sponsor/stakeholders. In practice, this may not be possible; however, some agreement needs to be reached in order for the next stages to be effective.

Who has this development need?

This question focuses on the learner and their current position. There is a series of secondary questions to be answered at this point:

- Is it an individual, team, department or organizational need?
- How many people in total have this need and where are they located?
- What are their positions, levels and job roles?
- What prior knowledge or experience has each learner got?
- What prior learning have they undertaken relating to this need?
- If there is more than one person with the need, are their needs the same or at different levels?
- How do the people with the need like to learn/learn most effectively?
- Are they aware that the need has been identified?

A word about prior knowledge and experience – identifying the starting point of the learner will enable you clarify whether the need is for new skills, new knowledge or new behavioural techniques. For example, the learner may have the knowledge of project management techniques, but they may not have the skills of team management or might not have managed an actual project – in this instance their development will require a method or methods that can help them learn the skills and behaviours required. Another learner may have managed a project, but not have the underpinning knowledge – in this case they require a method that allows them to learn the theories and concepts of project management. Sometimes it would appear that learners have the same need, but because of their prior knowledge, it is, in reality, a slightly different need.

The number and location of the learners will undoubtedly influence the choice of development method, as might their level within the organization – sometimes it is very difficult for a senior manager to be released from the business for any length of time; this also applies to solo posts where no cover is available.

Consideration should be given to the benefits and drawbacks of mixing different grades of staff. Benefits can be gained from working in a different environment where ranking is not an issue; however, individuals from 'lower' in the hierarchy may feel intimidated or limited by the presence of their managers.

Time

Understanding the deadline by which a person needs to implement their new learning and clarifying the time available for the learning to be undertaken is vital. Learning has to be undertaken as close to when it will be used as possible – the old adage 'use it or lose it' applies here. If it is not possible to arrange the development close to 'go-live', possibly because of the large number of people requiring the development, then opportunities for refreshers should be built into the plan.

A realistic assessment of how much time is available for the learner needs to be made, including how undertaking this development will impact on their 'day job' and their domestic arrangements. The best way of doing this is to ask the learner, rather than to make assumptions.

Prioritization

Whilst we would love to say that all development needs are important and should be met, let's get real! In the real world, there are limited resources which have to be apportioned appropriately. The correct way of prioritizing is to give preference to those learning needs that will have the biggest impact on the business and the achievement of its business plan – whether that is the organizational, department or team business plan. Remember though, this might not be the short-term plan. You may choose to do some career development for an individual who is key to the achievement of your business goals over the next two years, if the consequence of not doing it is that the person leaves the business this year. Also, when prioritizing, there may be legal considerations, such as equal opportunities, health and safety, or compliance.

If you have conducted an organizational learning needs analysis, it can be very effective to provide a development intervention as soon as possible so that people can see a commitment to acting on the results and a return on the time that they have spent providing the data. This is often termed a 'quick win'.

Organizational and environmental factors

Fundamentally, development is going to take place within the boundaries and context of the organization and therefore the starting point is to understand the culture of the organization and how it works. If you do not take into account the organizational context within which you are working then, at best, the development activities will be a struggle to implement and at worst they won't work at all. By understanding your organization you will be better able to select methods which are acceptable to and therefore supported by managers and staff alike.

It is helpful to have clarity about the following:

The organizational culture

Culture is defined by Robin Fincham and Peter Rhodes (1999) in *Principles of Organizational Behaviour* as 'the underlying values, beliefs and codes of practice that make a community what it is'. They go on to question whether organizations can be seen as having cultures given that they are made up of people from the surrounding community who bring their culture with them. However, they conclude that organizations are both 'part of and apart from society' and as such are 'communities in their own right, with distinctive rules and values'.

In other words, culture is 'the way we do things around here' – this covers not only the stated values, but custom and practice that exists within the organization or within different parts of the organization. Quite often there is a very different culture at Head Office than there is in the 'field'.

If you have been within the organization, you will already have established some thoughts on the culture through your own experiences and observations. Your perceptions can be validated and refined by discussing them with others (internally and externally) – how do they see it and what happens in practice? Reviewing decision-making practice, company policies and processes will also provide useful insight into the true culture – is it strict, autocratic, and standard-driven or is it more flexible and creative?

Cultures of organizations are affected, not just by their internal mechanisms, but also by the sectors in which they operate (eg type of industry and whether it is a public, private or not-for-profit organization) and the legislation/codes of practice by which they are bound. The historical context of the organization is an influential factor in how the culture develops and how easy it is to change the culture.

Questions to ask staff and stakeholders in order to help you identify the organizational culture:

- How do your managers manage you?
- How do you know what to do each day?
- What methods of communication are used within your organization?
- How do you know about changes within your organization?
- What do you know about this organization's strategies and plans for the future?
- What values and beliefs do you see in practice?
- Is this a unionized environment?
- How are people trained to do their jobs?
- How would you describe the atmosphere in this organization?

- What causes frustration in this organization?
- Who produces ideas in this organization?
- If this organization had a personality, how would you describe it?
- What is the catchment area for your recruitment activity?
- What sort of people do well in this organization?
- How does the organization treat individuals?
- How do people work together?
- How are decisions made in this organization?
- What happens when a mistake is made in this organization?
- How are people rewarded in this organization?
- What do your customers think of the organization?
- How high is staff morale?
- Are people proud to be part of this organization?

The organization's goals and objectives

Increasingly stated within the business plan, this is about where the organization intends to go in the short, medium and long term. It is important to have clarity around the issues affecting the organization, whether these are stated or not stated within the plan. For example, addressing staff turnover may not be stated within the business plan, but it could be a major issue which underpins improving productivity. Another example could be a downsizing project which would not necessarily appear in the business plan, but could be a means to achieving an objective which is about increasing profitability. Senior management teams do not always see these issues as important to development planning; however, they are important factors in ensuring that resources are appropriately allocated. There is, correctly, an increasing understanding that HRD should be integrated with the business, that it is not a functional responsibility that lies solely with a 'training department', but is 'everyone's' business and the development of staff operationally rests with the line managers.

The Investors in People (IiP) standard requires organizations to communicate their business plan to all staff and to link any development plans to the business plan. This has to be shown to work in practice and IiP assessors will ask individual members of the organization to demonstrate how their individual development objectives link back to the corporate goals and objectives.

In summary then, understanding the organization's goals and objectives allows you to:

1 identify areas for development;
2 prioritize development needs;
3 comply with the best practice as detailed in the IiP standard.

For some organizations, the goals and objectives may not be formally stated in a business plan, or they might be the sole preserve of the chief executive. However, all departmental heads and the executive team should know why their departments exist, what they should be doing and why, and where they are trying to get to. You may therefore need to have interviews with them in order to gain greater knowledge of their objectives, even if that means helping them to define them.

The organization's development history

This is important because it helps you establish the organization's learning style. It gives you the foundation on which to work – if you know what has gone before you can find out what worked or didn't work, what was deemed to be acceptable or not acceptable – and to build upon the successes or refine your approach.

What learning and development has been undertaken within the organization before? What impression has been left – what do people say about it? Has it been based on traditional skills training in classrooms? What impact have the learning and development activities had? Is training seen as something everyone should do or as a punishment for bad performance? How have development needs been identified in the past? What processes and practices are already in place for getting development – is it who shouts the loudest or based on assessed needs? What resources have been allocated to development in the past?

Stakeholders

Although not always acknowledged as part of the development planning process, knowing who the stakeholders are and what they envisage for the organization and its people is important as this enables you to have a full view of the context in which development will take place. For example, a parent company may wish to have all sister companies developing their managers together and in the same way, while another may allow each individual company to procure its own management development. Additionally, these people may also have views on what the development needs for the organization are and the priority that should be given to them. Stakeholders include: customers, suppliers, clients, service users, shareholders, governing bodies, government departments, the general public and so on, depending on the type of organization that you are.

Gathering stakeholder views can be achieved via focus groups, questionnaires, interviews, informal meetings, feedback such as complaints, and parent company plans.

People

This is about understanding the people resource of the organization. It is about understanding the people who make up the organization as a whole rather than individuals. It is about gathering relevant data such as gender, ethnicity, disability, operational staffing levels, age, number of people at each grade, educational standards, and their expectations for learning. Some of this information will come out of the research on culture. You will also need to understand what people management processes are in place, collective agreements that affect development, consultation processes, reporting mechanisms and organizational structures. This information is useful for monitoring and ensuring equality of opportunity in relation to choosing and providing learning and development methods – the information should be used to include, rather than exclude, people from learning and development activities.

Establishing information about the human resources of the organization helps you to establish what is expected or will be acceptable to the staff en masse. For example, individuals who belong to professional bodies with CPD requirements are more likely to have expectations of the organization in terms of what will be provided for their development. Another example would be in jobs involving high-risk activities where job holders have an expectation that refreshers will be provided for them on an ongoing basis. It will also give you foresight to the sort of questions or blocks that may be put in the way of the plans.

Environment

In this context 'environment' refers to the operating context of the organization. Factors to take into account are:

- The working patterns of the employees, eg night working, shift working, weekend working.
- Seasonal fluctuations in workload.
- The availability of short-term replacements if the methods chosen take the learners away from their workplaces.
- The 'political' situation of the organization, which may make some development methods inappropriate to use, eg an organization that has recently made staff redundant would be unwise to support a group of senior managers attending a conference on the other side of the world, unless there were clear business gains.
- Physical location of learners – cost and time of getting them together, coupled with the organizational policy on 'green' issues.
- Corporate and social responsibility strategy/environmental policy – can you link the organizational development activities to these strategies? For example, use secondments to charities or initiate projects that assist the community as well as achieve development objectives; select methods that are environmentally friendly, such as using internet discussion boards rather than having large numbers of people travelling long distances to attend an event.

Budget

How much money is there to pay for instruction, additional staff, equipment, support materials, venues and/or travel and subsistence? Who is paying for this – the organization, the department or the individual? Is there any funding available such as government funding, grants or career development loans? Budget or lack of it could be a major factor in your choice of development method, although some of the ones we have included in Chapter 4 can be wrapped into departmental operational budgets rather than a separate 'training and development' budget.

The costs of a development method can be calculated by adding the following elements:

- the costs of the person/people leading the activity or event (trainer, facilitator, coach, mentor etc);
- the costs of the learner(s) (salary, on-costs, cost of cover staff);
- travel and subsistence costs for learner(s) and the activity leader;
- costs involved with analysing needs and designing the development intervention;
- venue and accommodation costs, including lighting, heating, food, council tax etc;

- resource costs, eg production, purchase or hiring of materials;
- opportunity costs – the costs of the learner not carrying out their normal duties and the costs of anything else that the money or resources might have been used for;
- administration and marketing costs.

In Chapter 7, we return to this subject when we discuss cost–benefit analysis.

Resources

These are the people and physical resources that are available to you in planning development, including: time, facilities, space, colleagues and equipment. These may be internal to the organization; external resources can be purchased or rented such as additional space or facilitators. It is important to get a good overview of your resources before making decisions on methods, as you do not want to make a plan and then discover you haven't the resources to achieve that plan.

In Chapter 4, a number of the methods that we have described involve utilizing colleagues and other members of the organization as learning resources. All people have the potential to help others learn, but not all people can help others learn. In other words, anyone with a skill, piece of knowledge or behavioural technique could share that with another person; however, it is not as easy as just picking the first person as actually they need to have the following attributes:

- an appropriate level of competency in the skill, knowledge or behaviour to be learnt;
- effective interpersonal skills;
- some knowledge of how others learn and develop;
- willingness to be involved and to share their knowledge and skills;
- time – for planning, delivering and evaluating.

In addition to these attributes, the chosen person needs to have a belief that they will gain from the process – either they will develop themselves as a result of helping someone else, or there is some other reward, perceived or real. Consideration also needs to be given to their existing relationships with the learner, eg a line manager might not be the best person to coach a member of their team.

And finally...

It is temping to select methods solely on the basis that they worked for you, they use the latest technology or because they are fashionable at the moment. Don't do it! If it succeeds, it will be by accident rather than design. If it fails, not only has the learner not achieved their objectives, but you potentially have damaged the reputation of learning and development within your organization, as well as wasting valuable resources. Working systematically will provide you with factual evidence should it be needed to gain management support for a programme or to back up your decisions at some point in the future. Whilst it may seem time-consuming to go through this checklist, and at times your organization may demand a rapid solution which prevents proper analysis and planning, using this approach will ensure a higher quality of development and learning.

The following case study shows how Girlguiding UK selected the most appropriate methods for their learners and how ongoing review led them to change the methods to meet the needs of their members. They considered the culture, the mission and purpose of the organization as well as the personal needs and expectations of their members in deciding to use a competency-based approach.

Girlguiding UK – Competency-based Learning and Development Case Study

Contributed by Ann Matthews, Adult Support Section, Girlguiding UK

Girlguiding UK is the UK's largest voluntary organization for girls and young women led by women, with over 60,000 female volunteers aged between 18 and 65 working directly with the young members.

'Girlguiding UK, as part of a worldwide movement, enables girls and young women to fulfil their potential to take an active and responsible role in society through its distinctive, stimulating and enjoyable programme of activities delivered by trained volunteers' (Mission Statement, *The Guiding Manual* 4th Edition (2004)).

An issue for Girlguiding UK is how to deliver learning and development opportunities to the 60,000 volunteers in a practical and meaningful way that helps develop the individual as well as give them the knowledge, skills, values etc to deliver the aims of the organization. It is also important that as an organization Girlguiding UK recognizes the many talents and skills volunteers bring with them as well as providing opportunities for volunteers to learn new skills and develop existing skills in an enjoyable way. Girlguiding UK aims to offer its volunteers the chance to make a personal contribution to the future of girls and young women and, at the same time, to widen their own horizons.

In order to meet this aim, Girlguiding UK offers a range of training opportunities to all its adult volunteers. Some of these lead to formal qualifications which are recognized within and outside Girlguiding UK. Wherever possible, qualifications of other relevant bodies, particularly those of a more practical nature such as climbing and water activities, are recognized.

Where no suitable organization or qualification exists, Girlguiding UK provides its own training schemes and qualifications, all of which are competency based. Experience shows that volunteers develop much better in a 'learning by doing' environment.

This competency approach allows volunteers to be recognized for what they are already doing and requires little or no extra time for those who are already giving their time freely. The majority of our new volunteers are attached almost immediately to a Rainbow, Brownie, Guide or Senior Section Unit and this approach allows them to begin developing skills, gaining experience and collecting evidence of this immediately. Once they have completed the Girlguiding UK Leadership Qualification, which is mandatory, many want to move quickly on to taking their unit members on residential experiences, adventurous activities or any of the other wide range of opportunities Girlguiding UK offers its members. It is important that as an organization we harness this enthusiasm and do not put volunteers off by requiring that they attend training courses, read books etc when they could get 'qualified on the job'!

In the past Girlguiding UK operated a more flexible scheme for its adult volunteers, which lacked clarity. This led to individuals either being asked to 'jump through hoops' or being appointed to their role or awarded a qualification with little or no support or evidence that they could in fact 'do the job'. This in turn led to differing standards throughout the UK and in 1996 Girlguiding UK agreed that as new qualifications and schemes were introduced they would be delivered using the competency-based approach.

Girlguiding UK reviews its own qualifications and schemes on a three-yearly cycle and evidence shows that, providing there is adequate support from a mentor or assessor, volunteers are comfortable with the approach. There are still areas of concern regarding the amount of support each individual receives and also the amount of evidence some mentors require their candidate to produce. This is tackled by regular updates in the *guiding magazine*, through the nine Countries and Regions that make up Girlguiding UK and via regular learning and development opportunities and sessions.

In addition to producing internal competency-based qualifications and schemes, in 1996 Girlguiding UK became an approved centre for the then RSA (Royal Society of Arts) delivering the '520 Training and Development Award'. With the development of OCR (a merger of awarding bodies Oxford, Cambridge and RSA), Girlguiding UK maintained its centre status and is currently delivering the recently introduced Learning and Development Standards.

Whilst the provision of an externally recognized award provides Girlguiding UK's 800+ volunteer trainers with personal benefits such as an opportunity to develop their career via guiding, being an approved centre can be time- consuming and a drain on already limited funds. However, being an external award it is easier to standardize as there are criteria set down by OCR as the awarding body which must be met to maintain the centre status. The regular visits by the External Verifier ensure that once standards are met they are maintained and indeed improved upon. Despite this, there are issues around evidence and assessment which require constant monitoring by the Internal Verifiers to ensure that the standard does not slip at a more local level.

There is also the problem that as an organization Girlguiding UK has no control over the content of the standards when they are amended or, as more recently, completely changed. However, as a large organization Girlguiding UK are often consulted. The current standards meet the needs of Girlguiding UK; however, future standards may not and then the organization will have to seek a suitable alternative qualification or create its own, which will be time-consuming and costly.

Despite all of the issues that surround the competency-based approach, Girlguiding UK still believes that offering this form of learning not only personally develops the volunteer but also has an impact on retention. Each volunteer should feel that they are getting something in return for the time they are giving up that they can use outside guiding. Many of the volunteers that join Girlguiding UK have not had a good learning experience and this form of learning can often lead to a return to the learning environment, which is a positive message for recruitment and retention as well as for seeking external funding.

6

Development Plans: Theory into Practice

The earlier parts of this book have discussed the different learning and development methods available to you and suggested ways in which you can make decisions about which methods to use based upon a learning needs analysis and other organizational factors. Here we focus on how these different methods can be, and have been, used in real life. Some of the examples are in the format of case studies, others are written as development plans.

DEVELOPMENT PLANS

In this context a development plan is the strategy for achieving agreed learning outcomes. It brings together the learning objectives/outcomes with the methods and resources that will be used to achieve the outcomes, providing a plan of action for the learners and their managers. A good development plan includes: the required outcome against which the success of the activity will be measured; the development method or methods that will be undertaken; the resources required and the review or completion dates, ie the 'who', 'what', 'when', 'how' and 'where' of the learning activities.

We have identified three levels of development plans:

1 organizational;
2 departmental;
3 individual.

Organizational development plans

At this level the development plan provides an overview of the learning and development activities that have been identified to meet the general needs across the organization. They are often the output of a corporate learning needs analysis, which is frequently coordinated by the HR department and is used in budget preparation. Because they are often prepared in isolation and on an annual basis, they can become redundant documents that are viewed as a paper exercise. In an ideal world an organizational development plan will not be created until the business plan has been completed and a subsequent organizational learning needs analysis, relating to the business plan, has been carried out. It should then be reviewed on an ongoing basis against the current needs of the business – it is a requirement of Investors in People that you demonstrate 'how learning and development activities will help achieve organizational objectives and how you will measure their impact'.

An organizational plan includes the learning needs arising from the corporate business plan and the information gained from individual and team development plans. Following are three case studies which illustrate different organizational development plans. This is not to say that all needs are dealt with centrally; more often than not, centrally driven learning and development activities will be in response to corporate or organizational needs; specifically, they address the 'needs of the masses'. Increasingly, individual development has to be done at a local level in order to truly meet the individual's needs and therefore responsibility has been devolved (formally or informally, spoken or unspoken) to the line manager and the individual. This is where the non-traditional learning methods come into their own. (See Table 6.1.)

Although we have stated that organizational plans cover general needs, there are occasions when a subject-specific plan will be needed. This may be as a result of an organization-wide project or a review of specific skills and knowledge, such as IT, product knowledge or management skills. Figure 6.1 gives an example of this.

Table 6.1 An organizational development plan

Business Objective (from business plan)	Learning Needs	Departments/ Who	Numbers	Development Activity	Responsibility	Deadline/ Due Date
Decrease sickness absence by 25%	Knowledge of absence management procedures	All line managers, including team leaders	100	10 × 1-day training course	HR	By Dec 200x
				Self-study via intranet – procedures section	Learners	Prior to attending the course
	Skills to carry out return to work interview			Coaching	HR/Managers	Within a month of attending the course
Introduce new computer system with no more than a 5% loss of productivity for the first 3 months	Basic PC skills	All staff who do not pass competency assessment	400 – estimate	40 × 0.5-day introduction to PCs E-learning On-the-job training (floor-walkers)	HR Learners/floor-walkers	Jan–June 200x
	Operation of relevant parts of company system	All staff	820	Training courses – length depending on individual role, see separate plan On-the-job training (floor-walkers) Practise simulations on dummy system	HR Floor-walkers Line managers	May–Sept 200x
	Knowledge of new procedures and work processes	All staff	820	Team briefings E-learning assessment	Business analysts Line managers Learners	June–Sept 200x

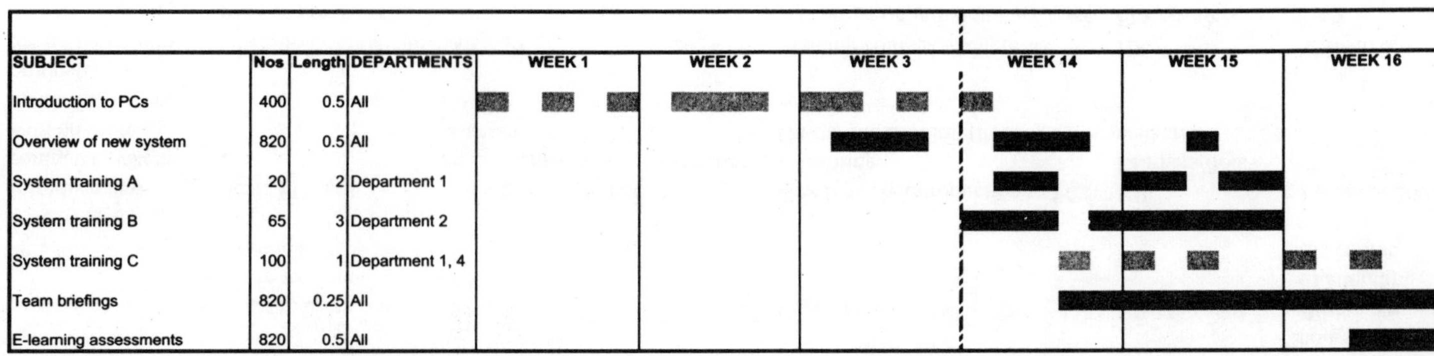

Figure 6.1 A subject-specific development plan

Case study 1: Absence management skills at Three Valleys Water Ltd

Three Valleys Water is the largest water-only supply company in the UK, operating to the north and west of London. It is owned by Veolia Water UK, part of the Veolia Environnement Group. Three Valleys Water provides over 800 million litres of water each day to over 3 million customers.

Between 2004 and 2005, the company successfully combined formal training with coaching and on-the-job learning to develop their managers' ability to manage absence. In this case study, Greg Jackson, HR manager, explains why they went for this multi-pronged approach and the results gained. Thanks are also given to Keith Luxon, the current Director of HR at Veolia Water.

In January 2004 the company became aware that there was an increasing trend in absence rates overall. A study showed that in 2002 direct absence costs for Three Valleys were in the region of £562,000 (3.6%) compared with an increase in 2003 to £712,000 (4.0%) and continuing to rise. These figures showed an upward trend of direct costs only; if indirect costs were also taken into consideration, it would be reasonable to assume that the actual overall costs would be potentially double the direct costs. This was compared to the average industry absence rates, as reported by the CBI in 2003, of 3.2% for the UK and 3.9% for the public sector.

On examining the absence statistics in detail it appeared that the majority of the problem was in the operational side of the business where the actual absence rate averaged 5.0%.

The specific issues were as follows:

- Generally high sickness levels, with a high number of individuals off long-term sick.
- High number of individuals appeared to be carrying out light duties or were not fulfilling the role that they were actually employed to do.
- No policy or guidelines were in place to enable and support managers to manage absence.
- Managers appeared to lack confidence or know how to deal effectively with absence issues.
- Managers had never received any formal training or coaching.

NEXT STEPS

It was clear that more information was required to understand the full extent of the problem and data was gathered from across the business to ascertain the specific status of individuals, whether they were sick, long-term sick, absent for other reasons, actually fulfilling their role etc.

FINDINGS

The collection of further data confirmed that the majority of the problem was in the operational side of the business, also that most of the sickness was due to a high number of employees being off long-term sick and not short term. What became apparent was that there were an extremely high number of employees working but not fulfilling the actual role that they were employed to carry out. Some employees were on light/lighter duties due to various health issues. It appeared that these employees had been off work and had returned on light duties and had never been managed back to carrying out their full role.

The fundamental issue was that managers did not have the knowledge, understanding or confidence to be able manage absence effectively.

The data indicated that a staggering 20 per cent of the operational workforce were either short-term or long-term absent or simply not fulfilling their full role. At this time, operations were also experiencing difficulties with resource availability; this is not surprising considering that 20 per cent of operational staff were either absent or not fulfilling their full role.

Therefore the decision was taken to focus on managing the long-term absence and capability issues.

MANAGING THE ABSENCE

The 'real' absence and capability state was presented and discussed with the company directors and agreement was obtained to manage the problem and reduce the absence and capability figures. This was to be driven by HR through line managers with the following actions:

- A Managing Absence Policy was written together with supporting guidelines for managers.
- A Managing Absence Workshop was designed and delivered to every manager and team leader in the business, the first audience being the trade unions. This provided the knowledge and understanding to enable managers to begin to tackle the issues. It was apparent from the workshops that managers were unclear as to how absence and capability issues should be managed; very positive feedback was received about the content and delivery of the workshops. The feedback indicated that the workshops alone would not be enough to enable managers to hit the ground running and have an immediate impact on dealing effectively with the absence issues. Managers indicated that they were under pressure to deliver the operational aspects of the role and that managing absence and capability was not an integral part of their day-to-day duties and therefore was generally tagged on to their everyday activities. The workshops did demonstrate that concentrating more time on managing and resolving

absence issues would in fact improve the amount of resource available and assist them in meeting operational targets. Therefore the Human Resources team dedicated a resource to support managers.

- It was found that the workshops had been useful in providing the knowledge and process for managing absence but what could not be passed on effectively to managers was the language and behaviours required actually to tackle the many 'difficult' cases and ensure that absence was consistently dealt with in the most appropriate way for each situation. It was for this reason that the decision was made to provide the resource to coach and 'hand hold' the managers through the many and sometimes difficult circumstances to either get individuals back to work fulfilling their duties or move them out of the business. Without this coaching it is felt that managers would have attended the training and been clearer on the process and guidelines but not fully confident or willing to deal with the many complex and difficult cases.
- As well as the training and coaching provided, other changes were put in place such as introducing a new occupational health provider together with the introduction of return-to-work interviews and home visits.
- Human Resources continued to coach the business through all of the sickness and capability issues and as a result many individuals either left the company or returned to carrying out their full duties.

CURRENT SITUATION

- Managers are now equipped and have the confidence to manage absence and capability issues effectively and are now taking ownership for managing absence. The Managing Absence Policy was agreed with the trade unions and is now used as a framework and guidance for all. Human Resources continue to support managers but to a far lesser extent as they now have the confidence and guidelines to enable them to manage absence and capability effectively.
- A small number of Managing Absence Workshops continue to be delivered as a refresher and for new managers.
- As a consequence of the drive to reduce absence levels some managers now have this as a measure on the balanced scorecard.
- Long-term absence and capability in operations has fallen from 20% to 3%.
- Absence rate fell from 4.3% in July 2004 to 2.8% in July 2005, with a reduction in direct absence costs over the same period of £105,000.

It is felt that this progress would not have been made in such a short space of time if the company had relied purely on delivering the training and guidelines to managers and leaving them to get on with it. Providing the ongoing coaching, support and advice enabled managers to manage the absence/capability cases confidently. Absence and capability cases often have to be dealt with according to the specific circumstances for each case and it would have been difficult to pass on the required skills purely through a training intervention. Providing the coaching and support by dealing with real 'live' issues and not just case studies in the classroom has genuinely increased the skill and knowledge in managing absence effectively.

Case study 2: Meeting the development needs of a small business

ABC Printing is a small business with six employees. The managing director started the company three years ago with one member of administrative staff and one operational employee. The business now employs an additional administrator who is responsible for bookkeeping and accounts, a sales executive and a total of 2.5 operational staff.

The MD and her team have produced the annual business plan which includes three main objectives:

1. Expand the client base from 25 clients to 40 clients.
2. Increase turnover by 10%.
3. Increase profit by 5%.

In order to achieve the business goals the following actions have been identified:

- Develop web-based trading.
- Employ an extra full-time sales executive.
- Install a computer-based client management system.

A number of development needs have been identified, resulting from the business plan:

1. Operational staff: increased business awareness is needed so that all employees understand the context of their work and the needs/requirements of their clients.
2. Administrative and sales staff: these employees will need to learn how to operate the new computer package and be able to manage the web-based trading system.
3. Accounts clerk: because the attention of the administrator will be focused upon the new computer system, this individual needs to take over credit control and therefore learn all aspects of this job.
4. New sales executive: this person is likely to come from a non-printing background, but will have solid and proven sales skills; therefore their development needs will be mainly about the business.

5 Managing director: the MD has identified that she needs to learn more about the legislation involved in employing people, specifically health and safety and employment law.

With help of her mentor, the managing director has drawn up a development plan which covers all of the identified needs. She has allocated a budget and identified priorities.

THE DEVELOPMENT PLAN

In order of priority:

1 Credit control: the accounts clerk will immediately begin shadowing the administrator to gain background knowledge of this aspect of his job prior to undertaking on-the-job training. The administrator has already gained on-job training skills from his previous employer.
2 Business awareness: a rolling programme of client visits for the operational staff has been set up to take place across a 12-month period. This has been planned so as not to clash with known busy periods and staff holidays. Meetings have been scheduled between the MD and each operational employee immediately following the visits to discuss their learning.
3 User training: the software house that will be supplying the client management system and the web-based trading system offers on-site training as part of their package. This will be delivered as part of the implementation programme. The administrator and sales executive will be allocated specific time to practise using the systems and discuss their experiences and learning.
4 MD development: the MD is a member of a local business networking group and plans to use this group to find herself a mentor from another business sector who has extensive experience of employing staff. She will also subscribe to an internet-based service to receive regular legislative updates.
5 New employee: an induction programme will be prepared for the new sales executive once the recruitment process has been completed. It will include coaching from the existing sales executive, client visits and planned time with the MD.

Departmental/team development plans

These are similar to organizational plans, but address the needs of a specific area within the organization. They will include information gained from individual development reviews as well as being linked to the departmental or team goals and objectives. Learning needs analysis tools such as skills matrices, direct observation and quality assurance data will also be useful inputs. Whilst these plans are the responsibility of the department manager, occasionally mangers may ask for a learning and development specialist to help review needs and advise on potential solutions.

These become one of the prime sources of input to central development plans, and are often more useful to central planners than individual development plans, as they can provide a summary of numbers, subject areas and importance to the department, rather than lots of personal data.

Case study 3: Multi-skilling call centre agents

A financial services company, which we will call Moneybank, was concerned about the standard of their customer service department; this arose from poor telephone response rates and increased customer complaints. A review of the team's skills matrix (see Figure 6.2) showed gaps in several areas, including product knowledge, complaints procedures and communication skills. The team leader reviewed the skills matrix and found that different individuals presented different gaps in skills and knowledge; this led to the development plan incorporating peer support and action learning sets.

Updated based on performance review meetings and quality checks by the call centre manager and team leaders.

0 = no competency
1 = requires supervision
2 = competent and able to perform without supervision
3 = able to train others

Name	Product A	Product B	Verbal Communication	Complaints Handling	Systems	Written Communication
AY	1	2	3	0	3	2
JC	1	2	3	0	3	2
SJ	1	2	3	0	3	2
JT	2	2	1	0	3	1
KZ	2	2	1	1	3	1
GC	2	2	1	1	3	1
ST	1	1	2	1	3	2
EC	1	1	2	2	3	2
ET	3	1	3	3	3	2
VB	3	1	2	3	3	1
NH	3	3	3	1	2	2
NG	2	0	2	0	2	1
IO	2	0	1	0	2	2
MKL	2	3	1	3	2	2
MFL	0	3	3	3	2	3
HW	0	3	2	3	2	3
SB	0	1	3	3	1	3

This skills matrix shows that the biggest needs for the team are in complaint handling and knowledge of product A.

Figure 6.2 The Moneybank Call Centre skills matrix and training plan

Training Plan

Subject	Priority	Learner	Method to address need	Facilitator/supporter	When
Complaint handling (to bring up to level 2)	1	ST, NH	Secondment to complaints section.	Complaints section team leader	Now
Written and verbal communication (to bring up to level 2)	1	JT, KZ, GC	Project to establish standard letters and paragraphs on the system and to review the 'call scripts' currently being used.	Team leader	Now
Product A (to bring up to level 2)	2	AY, JC, JT, ST, EC	Self-study using intranet and company information. Assessment of knowledge by VB.	VB	Over next 3 months
Product B (to bring up to level 2)	2	EC, ET, SB	Self-study using intranet and company information. Assessment of knowledge by MFL.	MFL	Over next 3 months
Complaint handling (to bring up to level 1)	3	AY, JC, SJ, NG, IO	Shadowing of individuals with grade 3 in this area.	MKL and HW	Over the next 2 months

Figure 6.2 *continued*

Case study 4: Using NVQs as a team development tool

With thanks to Geoff Coughlin, Director Emphasis on Skills Ltd (www.emphasisonskills.com)

THE PROJECT

This NVQ project involved Emphasis on Skills Ltd providing Level 3 NVQ Award programmes for a training team of seven individuals, all working for a national construction company. Although managers, they deliver a significant number of training events that cover both technical training and skill development at all levels within the organization.

DRIVERS FOR THE PROJECT

- *Accountability.* The organization had been the subject of at least one Inquiry into their service delivery and accountability had arisen as a key issue. Individual managers had been asked what qualified them to provide the training and development activities for the workers directly involved in the incident that led to the Inquiry. It emerged that although the manager-trainers were recognized internally as competent and highly skilled practitioners and managers, they didn't have formal qualifications to demonstrate their competence as trainers.

  By undertaking an NVQ award programme, the organization could then *prove* that their trainers were at a good level of expertise and competence – a key element as far as accountability is concerned.
- *Improved safety.* Safety issues were also a relevant driver. This organization was required to operate its activities safely and to provide relevant training in this respect. It was felt that if the organization could demonstrate that their trainers were delivering to externally monitored and nationally recognized standards, then this should have a direct influence on improving safety within the organization.
- *Consistency of training delivery.* This project additionally provided an opportunity for these and other quality assurance managers to check on the overall quality of the training and development activities provided internally. Everything from training session plans to presentations was affected in some way by this project, with activities being aligned to the national standards within the award. The specific performance criteria and evidence requirements within each unit provided direction and focus.
- *Maximizing the use of existing qualifications.* The organization felt exposed and vulnerable to the criticism levelled at it and decided to ensure that all seven managers affected became qualified to train and be recognized to

national standards of competence. Importantly, following some internal needs analysis it transpired that several already held D32 and D33 assessor units (replaced by the A1 unit) within the learning and development NVQ framework. Following consultation, the organization was able to recognize that these units could form the start of a tailored NVQ training and assessment programme for the managers, culminating in the achievement of a Level 3 qualification in learning and development.

Using trainers' existing qualifications also had a significant motivational effect on the managers. Very positive feedback was received at an early stage confirming this fact. Individuals were clearly impressed at not being asked or 'made' to repeat tasks and activities in which they had already been deemed to be competent.

THE PROGRAMME

Having agreed which 'core' and 'optional' units each manager-trainer was going to undertake, a timescale was agreed for completion. This was and is often important organizationally in order to prevent slippage and focus on the task in hand, which was to get everyone to the required standard quickly and within a reasonable time. In the event six out of seven achieved their qualification within twelve months. The final member of the group received certification for five of the units – their role changing towards the end of the programme.

There were several factors that contributed towards the success of this programme:

1 *Using day-to-day work as evidence*. This is key to successful NVQ programmes – especially when the individual has to produce evidence. Using simulated activities is not allowed in the NVQ framework and so real work situations provided individuals with their opportunity to gather the performance and documentary evidence required to demonstrate competence. The whole evidence-gathering process is much easier when people can use the everyday resources around them.

2 *Training to support the programme*. This is something that is often overlooked when organizations are looking to support individuals on their NVQ programmes. It is important to realize that the units and awards are assessment tools to establish the competence of individuals. They don't *develop* individuals per se, although invariably there is development to a greater or lesser extent. Individuals so often need help with the 'how to' side of things; knowing 'what' they have to do frequently isn't sufficient to ensure success and achieve the wider aims of the organization outlined above.

The client recognized that some individuals needed training input to expand their knowledge and learning. Examples included presenting, instructing and coaching skills. Sufficient time was set aside for trainers to deliver sessions - usually half and full days spread throughout their programme and supporting each unit. The session materials became useful sources of evidence to support the knowledge requirements for each unit.

3 *External quality assurance.* This has to be one of the advantages of using an NVQ provider from outside the organization. Of course, the nature of your own organization, which may well have large numbers of 'candidates' (individuals undertaking their NVQs), may well motivate you to become a 'centre' - able to certificate individuals on behalf of the Awarding Body, in this instance City & Guilds. City & Guilds has robust quality assurance procedures, as does Emphasis on Skills. In addition to the quality assurance factors included in the above points, it was also a key element of the results.

RESULTS OF THE PROGRAMME

This programme produced the following results:

- Increased confidence of the group of managers in their training skills.
- A measurable improvement in the quality of training identified through evaluation activities.
- One of the managers decided to retrain to become a professional trainer.
- Improved credibility of the training provided by the team to their staff.
- Production of evidence of a quality assured programme of training, which could be used if an Inquiry arose again in the future

Individual development plans

These are detailed action plans containing information about what an individual will do to meet their learning needs. Within the workplace, these are usually the product of dialogue between the individual and their manager, via appraisal or personal development review processes. However, some organizations provide staff with 'development' advisers who are not their line managers, and some individuals will be able to create their own plans. For individual development plans to be successfully carried out within the workplace, the line manager will need to agree and support the plan.

Broadly speaking, there are two levels of individual development plan – the high-level plan which covers all the currently identified needs and a longer-term proposal for how these will be met; and a micro plan which takes each individual need and details the specific steps to be taken to achieve the required outcome(s). Line managers and individuals should be wary of putting too many different needs and outcomes on one plan, or trying to address too many different development needs at one time, as this may lead to time conflicts, confusion about priorities or just scare the learner. We recommend that learners limit themselves to addressing between one and three needs at any one time, depending upon the depth and breadth of the need, and their other commitments.

Individual development plans can be an excellent motivational tool; however, they can also raise expectations that the organization will not be able to fulfil. Again, this is where development methods that can be built into the individual's or team's work can be beneficial – methods such as self-study, shadowing, delegation, on-the-job training etc can be arranged by the manager and/or individual themselves, without the need for central budget or permission. These methods encourage the individual to take responsibility for their own development, which assists the learning process as the individual is likely to be more committed and focused. An example of an individual development plan is given in Figure 6.3.

Case study 5: Two approaches to the development of time management skills

Time management is one of the regular needs that crops up in most organizations, regardless of their sector or size. Here, we explore two different approaches that can be taken to developing time management skills. It is based on our experiences both as trainers of time management courses and as managers who have supported people in developing these skills. The names have been changed to protect the innocent!

THE CLASSIC APPROACH – THE TRAINING COURSE

Twelve people attended a one-day open training course, delivered by a well-known provider. Here is a little information about five of them and their development needs.

Joanne's need was identified during her performance review meeting with her manager, when they agreed that she was finding prioritizing her work difficult, especially when the requests came from other departments. She invariably found herself with too much work and didn't always work on the most pressing piece of work – often completing the item that she enjoyed most or the task requested by the most senior person. Consequently, she was booked onto the course with the external training company that the training department always used for this type of need. Joanne found the

Name:

Learning plan for the next 12 months

What do I want to learn?	What will I need to do to achieve this?	What resources or support will I need?	What will my success criteria be?	Target date for completion

Figure 6.3 A personal development plan

course enjoyable and the 65-minute session section on prioritizing according to importance and urgency very useful. The course also covered to-do lists, handling interruptions, diary management, delegating, saying no and meetings.

Bill is an experienced person who asked to attend the course as part of his development plan. Everyone in his company is expected to undertake 16 hours of training a year and when he and his manager reviewed the list of available courses, this seemed the best one, and after all, it was 8 or so years since he had been on a time management course. Bill told his manager afterwards that it was a good reminder to use to-do lists and plan the week. Oh yes, and lunch was good!

Frank was sent on the course by his organization, and admitted during the opening part of the day that he didn't really know why. His manager had put him on the course because Frank never seems to get around to responding to e-mails and his desk is untidy.

Generally Cheryl is a lovely person who is always late, for work, for appointments, for everything! She likes to talk to everyone and help them out whenever she can. Her manager talked to her about timekeeping and Cheryl explained that between taking the children to school and arriving at work she just 'nips into the dry cleaners, picks up gran's shopping lists, arranges for her nails to be done and rings her mum to ensure that she is able to pick up the children and take them to their after-school classes'. She is so nice and friendly that when she says 'I still get my work done, it's about being organized', her manager doesn't have the heart to tell her that being late three times a week or leaving early a couple of nights is a problem! And most of the time, she does get her work done, just as most of the time she takes a pile home with her at the weekend. They agreed on the time management course as 'you have a lot to plan into your life, Cheryl, and this might give you some ideas about planning'.

Robert is 22 and joined his firm as a trainee lawyer six months ago, having finished his degree. The course was identified as part of his induction programme – all graduates attend this and four other courses (Health and Safety, project management, negotiation skills, interpersonal skills).

Five weeks after the course, an evaluation of learning was completed.

Joanne had a one-to-one with her manager, two days after returning from the course, during which she spent about 10 minutes telling her how useful the course was and how she needed to classify her work by urgency and importance. Reassured that the training had worked, the manager moved on to the budget submission that was required by the end of that day. The meeting overran by 45 minutes!

Five weeks later and there seems to be no improvement in Joanne's performance; in fact she is feeling more frustrated than ever as she now finds that everything on her desk appears to be urgent! Her manager is constantly asking where work is.

For Bill, there was no measurable change in his performance or behaviour.

Frank found the programme useful and is trying to actively manage interruptions by asking people if he can talk to them later. His manager has noted that he is spending less time chatting during the middle of the day, but is disappointed that overall his management of paper and e-mails is not better, and often a week or more goes by before e-mails are responded to. His desk is still very untidy.

Cheryl came back from the course with lots of ideas. She bought a new organizer diary and now spends 20 to 30 minutes using it. She hasn't reduced the amount she is trying to fit in, nor has her timekeeping improved. Her planning is good, but still short term.

Robert, being naturally organized, found the course very useful and has been able to apply much of it with the help of his mentor. He now uses detailed to-do lists, and these feed into the time schedules he is expected to keep that inform client invoices. The most useful element of the course for Robert has been meeting management, and immediately after the course, he planned out how he was going to improve the meetings he was part of. With the help of his mentor, he has been following the action plan for the last five weeks, and has successful achieved 70 per cent of his learning goals. Last week, he organized a meeting that a senior partner attended, and the senior lawyer commented afterwards on how impressed he was with the pre-meeting briefing notes and the efficiency of the meeting.

A DEVELOPMENTAL APPROACH

For all these people (and we admit, we do not know what happened to the other six that attended the course!) the training course did not fully meet their learning needs. Robert only achieved his learning plan because he had help back in the company where he worked. There was nothing wrong with the course – it was well designed, properly delivered and even evaluated at the end. It was a good training course....

So what seems to have gone wrong? Some managers may think that it's their staff's fault – they have had the training and still haven't been able to improve. However, consider this for a moment. **They were given the wrong development!** A training course alone was never going to solve the issue. So here we offer an alterative approach.

For Joanne, the course provided her with the technique or theory to improve her prioritizing – but what she really needed was help in applying it to her situation and organization. She needed someone to help her identify the urgency of her work, and help her ask others when the work had to be completed by. Joanne had always worked for a company where if a manager asked you to do something, you didn't question it!

Therefore, an alternative approach would be for Joanne to attend the course and then to receive coaching.

Bill doesn't have a time management learning need; he is required to do 16 hours of development, but it would be more beneficial for him to keep up to date with industry developments by attending his engineering institution's meetings and conferences, reading industry magazines, and organizing team update meetings.

Frank's manager needs to give him feedback about those aspects of his performance that need improving so that they can have an honest conversation about how Frank can achieve it. It may be that simply being aware of his manager's concerns is sufficient for Frank to behave differently. Frank may need to attend the course to learn e-mail and paper management techniques; alternatively, he may be able to learn these by undertaking an e-learning programme, or shadowing a colleague who is good at these areas.

Cheryl actually needs someone to help her plan her work in detail – what she will do each day and what to do if she can't actually complete everything she has planned. Her manager can help this by managing her – if flexitime is not acceptable in her department, then he needs to tell her and explain the consequences of her continuing to do it. At the same time, he can tell her not to take work home. Ideally, her manager would be a good person to help her plan her daily and weekly work. She may also benefit from receiving coaching in how to become more assertive and saying 'no'.

Robert is a good example of how combining training with mentoring and an opportunity to use the skills in practice works well.

Case study 6: Personal development to improve leadership skills

Nina is an experienced and successful IT project manager for a large international transport and distribution company, based in the UK. She began her career 18 years ago as a business analyst, and she has always worked for the same company, becoming a project manager 6 years ago. She is one of their senior project managers. She has a very good knowledge of the company systems and has worked hard to learn the project management processes and techniques. She is considered by those around her to be good, getting results in difficult projects, if occasionally 'driven and focused'.

As part of a company-wide initiative to improve leadership skills, Nina attended the 'Leadership Programme' in September 2004. This was a modular programme delivered off-site at the organization's training school. The stated objectives of the course were that participants will:

1 be able to describe what effective leadership means in this organization and they will demonstrate it at work;

2 have improved self-awareness and know how to manage their impact upon others;
3 be able to develop and use informal communication networks and have enhanced their communication skills;
4 improve their personal capacity to lead and manage change.

Module 1 of the programme provided input on different styles of leadership, including 'transformational leadership', 'action-centred leadership' and 'situational leadership', all delivered in the context of the organization's own perceived leadership style. Module 2 of the programme was preceded by a 360-degree feedback process, during which Nina was able to receive some open, honest and constructive feedback which was discussed with her programme mentor (an experienced individual allocated by the training school as part of the programme). As a result of these discussions, Nina identified that she did not always relate to her team well – because she was very results-orientated, most of her communication with the team was around tasks and progress, thus some team members thought she was cold and not interested in their well-being. Two people in the 360-degree feedback process accused her of being a control freak! She left Module 2 of the programme with the following development plan:

Table 6.2

STOP	**WHY/HOW**
Chasing people for their next steps	Set objectives and agree review meetings – do not chase between meetings. Need to show the team that I trust them. Ask team members to tell me when I am doing it.
START	
Having 1:1s that involve feelings as well as the progress of tasks.	It's important to know how people are feeling about their work, not just whether the work is done or not. To help me, I will plan an agenda for these meetings.
Having lunch with the team	At least once every two months, to provide the opportunity to unwind, for everyone to get to know each other and also to talk informally about what is happening in the project and/or company.
CONTINUE	
Thanking people for their contribution	

Module 3 of the programme provided the opportunity to practise the leadership skills that had been covered previously through a series of outdoor activities and drama-based scenarios.

By the end of the programme Nina was able to identify that she was not a 'bad' leader – she had attended a number of management and leadership courses in the past and had successfully led several teams over the years. The course provided her with the opportunity to stand back and reflect upon her knowledge, skills and experience and how they applied to her current situation. Module 1 provided some theory and context, Module 2 provided, via the 360-degree feedback process, objective information about her performance and Module 3 gave the opportunity to practise some different behaviours in a 'safe' environment, where mistakes were not business-critical. The modular nature of the programme meant that the learning taking place could be applied to the workplace and embedded over a period of time. Attending the next module was impetus to complete action plans and this was reinforced by the provision of the programme mentor. As a result of participating in this programme, Nina identified ways she could develop as a manager, and these formed the basis of her ongoing development plan.

Case study 7: Manager as researcher

Colin Woodward

My decision to undertake a Master's degree was not generated through any great desire to become a more informed practitioner in my professional area. It was, probably in common with the majority of people undertaking this level of professional study, generated by a wish to improve my career prospects by adding something extra to my CV, hopefully giving me an edge over other candidates when applying for more senior roles. From my previous educational experience I certainly did not expect this to be a significant learning experience, one which would fundamentally change the way I thought and operated as a manager.

My previous educational background was limited to further education study on vocational subjects. Consequently, for the first 20 years or so of my working life my concept of 'learning' was the acquisition of the field of knowledge that the relevant professional bodies determined that I should know. The idea that one might go further than this, that one could generate knowledge for oneself through research and self-reflection, was an unknown. Perhaps I would have had more of an insight into this form of learning if I had undertaken a first degree, but my impression from graduates whom I have frequently recruited and worked with is that this is still something of a rare concept.

I am pleased to say that undertaking the Master's helped to deliver the outcome that I sought in relation to career progression. However, the skills that this period of study helped to develop have benefited my career in practical ways that extend beyond the simple polishing up of my CV.

The Master's degree that I undertook had a limited amount of taught content and this element of the programme was delivered through a small number of two or three days' residential sessions. The focus of these taught elements primarily built on the knowledge content of formal qualifications gained at either first-degree or postgraduate diploma level. This prior level of knowledge was a course entry prerequisite that enabled the primary focus of the assessment process to be focused on the completion of a 15,000–20,000-word dissertation relevant to the subject area; a typical format for this type of part-time study programme.

The dissertation was to be completed by researching a problem or issue in the organization that employed me at that time. This was to be carried out using an Action Research-based methodology. Whilst I believe that I developed a number of skills during this study, such as critical thinking, report writing, etc, the real benefit came through developing an understanding of Action Research and the skills to use some of the tools associated with it.

A professional researcher would be happy to detail the different approaches that are encompassed within the broad title of Action Research. For the purpose of this discussion, it is sufficient to explain that it is an approach that is grounded in the reality of the phenomenon that it sets out to explore. It does not require the researcher to look at an existing situation and propose in advance a theory which explains what is happening, ie I can see a problem over here and I think it is because X does Y which leads to Z. This 'hypothesis' approach then requires the researcher either to prove or to disprove the hypothesis by carrying out the research. Whilst this is a well-accepted and proven technique, from the point of view of the manager as researcher, this provides some significant problems. It is difficult to introduce this approach into looking at work-based problems as part of the manager's day job, either as part of a formal study programme or as a technique for problem solving in more general terms. In carrying out your research, should your hypothesis prove to be wrong, it would be difficult to justify the time and effort taken, although from a purely academic point of view this may be an acceptable outcome.

Action Research, by contrast, does not require the researcher to adopt a theory or hypothesis to test. It is possible to be more deductive in approach, enabling the researcher to say 'hey, I've got a problem over here, I don't know what is causing it so let's find out and *do something about it*'. This latter point is critical; the manager as researcher in an Action Research context has an obligation to change the situation, not simply to understand it. In addition, the manager as researcher does not walk away from the subject matter after the intervention has taken place. The manager usually remains in place in the organization and is able to assess the effectiveness of any intervention or initiative that has been taken to address the problem situation. This provides extra insights into the 'whole system' concept of the organization and enables action to be taken if the system reacts adversely to the intervention.

The more cynical amongst you may look at this and observe that this is simply a repackaging of the age-old management process of 'do, observe and correct'. In many ways this is true. However, by undertaking at least one research project using an Action Research methodology, with the added rigour of being formally supervised through carrying this out as part of a study programme, the manager benefits in a number of ways.

Firstly, the manager develops familiarity with a number of research techniques and the understanding of how and when to use them. Secondly, by working with an academic supervisor on your research, formal writing skills can be greatly improved. In my experience it is rare to receive feedback on written work once you have left school and the supervision process sharpens the researcher's ability to communicate succinctly. I've worked in both private and public sectors and the ability to make your point quickly and justify it with evidence is an important skill for managers at all levels. With an increasing emphasis on corporate governance and accountability, for senior managers it may well be a critical skill. Whilst some may find it difficult to accept that writing a 15,000-word dissertation can be training for business report writing, my belief is that the general principles hold good for both: know your audience, link the evidence to back up your conclusions and include only what is necessary.

The requirement to reflect and think about my own performance led to another benefit for me. I have always found negative feedback from others difficult to accept. My Master's project expected me to be more self-critical in approach, to formally consider what I might have done differently and what I have learnt. I have found that I do this more often now and in turn this has helped me to accept feedback from others. By identifying my own weaknesses I guess it has made it easier to accept it when I also hear it from others.

Finally, the completion of my Master's has given me more confidence in a number of ways. I am not fazed by the prospect of addressing significant workplace problems, whether that is by commissioning others to carry out the research or doing it myself. For example, I am currently commissioning a university to carry out a small research project looking at staff perceptions of access to career development opportunities, something that I would have had difficulty with prior to gaining my own experience. Also, I am no longer unsettled in working with others who have undertaken Master or Doctorate-level study. Working in the public sector, in the last six years I've worked with three chief executives who have completed Doctorates. Whilst my own study is not at that level, I feel more comfortable and confident in dealing with such people and feel more capable of holding my own when in discussion with them.

In conclusion, I believe that undertaking a research-based Master's has enabled me to develop a greater understanding of the organizations that I have worked for in all their complexity. The expertise developed in carrying out Action Research has provided additional confidence and ability to identify, analyse and manage problems as part of the organization as a system. In essence, when the iceberg is spotted on the surface, it provides the tools and techniques in a very practical way to dive below the surface and explore the greater mass underneath. It allows the manager to develop their skills by grappling with genuine problems, not working on simulations or case studies, and in my opinion, the concept of 'manager as researcher' should be seriously considered by most managers and organizations as part of a wider portfolio of management and career development.

7

Assessing the Impact

In this penultimate chapter of the book we will look at how to determine the success of learning and development activities. We discuss how learning and development can be evaluated and split this process into validation, evaluation and assessing the 'value-added' outcomes.

WHY ASSESS THE IMPACT?

If learning and development is to be placed high on the agenda of your organization, you must be able to demonstrate that it impacts the business. The impact may be linked to the achievement of the business plan (short or long term), the well-being of the employees or the reputation of the organization. Learning and development is not a 'nice to do', fluffy activity that exists for its own sake – it is a necessity if the organization is to survive and grow.

So how important is the process of evaluation? Many development specialists will make excuses for the lack of process by promoting the idea that the important thing is that development occurs and that people are continuously growing. In the current climate of leaner organizations there is a need to show how *all* activity within the organization is contributing to the business effectiveness – increasingly, companies and other organizations are reviewing everything that is done within all their departments against the achievement of their stated business purposes and goals. Too often learning and development activities have been cancelled or stopped because of a short-term requirement to save money, resulting in organizations that are unable to grow, compete or change. The validation and evaluation processes are important because organizations need evidence to prove that time, money and other resources dedicated to learning and development are well spent – that they are getting a return for their investment.

The other prime reason for evaluating learning activities, from our experience, is that it encourages others to undertake development – it shows commitment of individuals and their managers, and places the onus firmly on them – if you want to keep up, you need to participate.

It is impossible to stand still in current organizations, whether they be private, voluntary or public sector. By evaluation of development activities and promotion of the results of the evaluation, a range of individuals can be engaged in the process of learning. No one can say that they do not need to learn anything to do their job. Learning is essential at all levels – cleaning staff need to be aware of new Health and Safety legislation; sales staff need to continuously increase their product knowledge; technical staff need to keep up to date with the latest technological developments; administration staff need to be aware of data processing or new IT systems; managers need to increase their knowledge of employment law; operational staff need to be aware of new procedures; and senior managers need to have a good knowledge of all areas of their business.

It is difficult to isolate the effects of development – how much of what someone does is directly related to the development received or undertaken, and how much is caused by other factors? We are dealing with people and therefore other factors such as personality, experience, and other areas of life can impact someone's behaviour. The development may be the catalyst for change – however, change might be due, for example, to someone receiving feedback, growing up or having additional responsibilities such as a baby or a mortgage. Just having time to reflect may be enough – someone goes on a training course and it is not the training content that makes the alteration but just having the time away from the workplace and space to think results in them making a change. It is difficult, but not impossible.

HOW CAN THE IMPACT BE ASSESSED?

Quite often the impact of learning and development activities, especially training courses, is assessed simply by gathering participants' reactions – this is level 1 of Kirkpatrick's evaluation model which was created in 1994. Figure 7.1 is our interpretation of the model, shown as four overlapping circles to demonstrate the fact that each level of evaluation is important and the information gathered at each point will feed into each of the other levels. The importance of assessing the impact upon the organization is illustrated by placing this at the centre of the diagram.

In his article, 'Training programme evaluation', written for Business balls.com, Leslie Rae points out that 'even well-produced reactionnaires do not constitute validation or evaluation'. At best, it measures whether the person thinks the intervention has been of benefit. A positive reaction tends to indicate that there is more likelihood that they have learnt something and that they will implement or use that learning. A negative reaction might suggest that they have closed off to the experience and the learning. What it doesn't do is tell us anything about the achievement of the learning objectives or whether learning has taken place.

Validation

Validation is about measuring the achievement of learning and can be subdivided into pre- or post-event validation. Pre-event validation is a

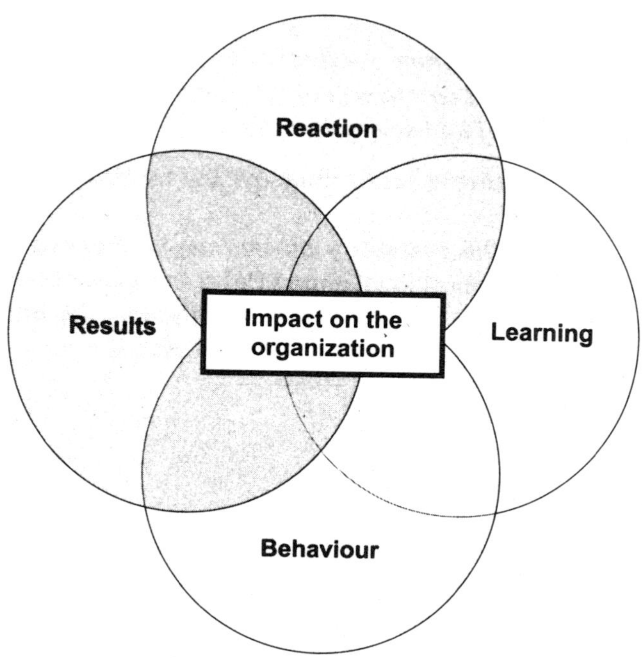

Figure 7.1 A diagrammatic interpretation of Kirkpatrick's evaluation model

check to ensure the learning objectives for the activity are a true reflection of the needs identified, and can be achieved by running pilot groups, asking stakeholders and sponsors or doing a simple self-check.

Post-event validation has two facets – the first is whether learning has occurred, and the second is whether the learning objectives have been achieved. This is the second level of Kirkpatrick's model.

In order to assess learning, you need to ask the question 'how will we know that the individual has learned this skill, knowledge or behaviour?' at the start of the development programme, and not wait until the end. The answer to this question may be that we are happy if the individual tells us 'yes, I have learnt', but some situations may require the learning to be tested by implementing some formal assessment procedures, eg end tests, or informal procedures such as observation in the workplace.

Assessing if any learning has occurred is much easier if you know the learners' level before they start the programme so that you can measure the difference at the end. This can be described as assessing entry and exit behaviours.

Evaluation

> *'Evaluation differs from validation in that it attempts to measure the overall cost benefit of the programme and not just the achievement of laid down objectives'.*
>
> Glossary of Training Terms, Employment Department, 1971

Kirkpatrick's model splits evaluation into two stages – Performance (level 3 of his model) and Organizational impact (level 4 of his model). We agree with those who add a third stage (which has become the fifth level in Kirkpatrick's model), that of Return on investment.

Performance

This level of evaluation is about measuring the effect of a learning experience on the individual's work/life (depending on the purpose of the programme). Has the person applied their learning so that it has changed the way in which they do things?

Once again, in order to measure the impact of a programme on individual performance it is essential to know what the performance was before the programme, so that changes can be measured. This level requires some quantitative measures of progress to be defined so that evidence can be gathered about the changes that have been made as a result of the learning. For example, a member of the cleaning team attends a briefing about the different colour-coding system associated with using cleaning equipment in different areas. The required outcome is that the individuals then use the appropriate equipment in the appropriate areas. This change in behaviour could be measured by observing the use of the equipment in the right place. A further example would be where a member of staff has the objective of learning more about a different department so that they can improve the flow of information between the two areas. The achievement of this can be assessed by getting them to make a presentation to other team members and then monitoring the flow of information over a fixed time period.

Changes in performance can be measured by quantitative data such as the number of errors or items produced; equally, it can be measured through observation, where changes in behaviour are seen or heard. This all comes back to what you expect to see when a job or task is carried out better than it was before the development took place.

Impact on organization

This is how the learning impacts or affects the organization as a whole, and is the first stage of evaluation that focuses away from the individual and on to the wider benefits. Prior to putting development in place, questions around what we expect the impact to be for the organization should be asked – this is easier if there is a measurable process, operational issue or mistakes to be overcome, for example reduction in rejection rates, better attendance or fewer complaints. However, sometimes organizational impact and results are/cannot be anticipated; unintended outcomes may come to light as a result of the evaluation.

This cannot take place at the same time as the development activity, but needs some time for the learner(s) to transfer their learning and use it in the real world. Measures have to be in place. It has to take place over a reasonable period of time – measuring for one week will not necessarily give the correct data. It is useful to have pre-development data to compare.

Return on investment (ROI)

This is the process of stating how much the development has cost against the returns for the organization – as a result of spending this amount we have seen these results. Ideally this is put in financial terms – for this £expenditure we get this £return – it is the cost–benefit analysis.

This part of the process is challenging as many benefits of development cannot be put into financial terms, although the costs of any development can be more easily measured.

The starting point for converting benefits to a monetary value is to identify what will change as a result of the learning and then break it down into 'units of data', eg error rates, customer complaints or satisfaction, product produced per hour, attendance, staff turnover, equipment break-downs, accident rates or formal grievances. You then take the following steps:

1 Put a monetary value, or cost, on each unit of data. This may be difficult to do and if this is the case, consultation with managers can help to produce an accurate estimate.
2 Calculate the difference in performance before and after the learning activity, eg how many errors were made before the event and how many are now being made. This should be measured over comparable periods so that you are comparing like with like, eg how many errors were made in a set period of time prior to the activity and how many errors were made in the same period of time following the activity. The longer the period of measurement, the more accurate the calculation will be.
3 Multiply the difference by the cost of each unit (calculated at 1) to give the final monetary benefit.

A simple example of calculating the value of benefit gained from a learning intervention

a = Number of errors before learning took place
b. = Number of errors after learning took place
c = Cost of each error
d = Difference in the number of errors taking place (= a–-b)
v = Value of the benefit gained as a result of the learning (= c × d)

If

a = 15 errors per month
and
b = 7 errors per month
then
d = 8 errors per month

Therefore if c = £2.50

v = £20 per month

The ROI can be calculated by taking the cost of the learning event from the total value of all identified benefits. You may find that it takes several months to gain a positive return on investment.

Techniques relevant to the different levels of evaluation

Table 7.1 illustrates the usefulness of the different methods of validation and evaluation for each of the different levels identified in Kirkpatrick's model.

ADDED VALUE AND UNINTENDED OUTCOMES

Very often, when learning and development plans have been completed, there are benefits and/or outcomes that you were not expecting – these are known as the 'value added' results. These results are not always quantifiable or even seen as being beneficial, but the organization will generally gain in the longer term. They may include:

- increased motivation of the learner, which may then have an impact on the motivation of the team as a whole;
- greater commitment to the organization, its values and its business goals;
- learners deciding upon a new career or life direction;
- new business ideas and products/services;
- organizational learning;
- improved communication, inside and outside the organization;
- changes to working procedures and practices;
- feedback from learners resulting in amendments to programmes and methods – or even discontinuing the programme altogether;
- increased ability to learn and improved critical-thinking/problem-solving skills;
- an increase in flexibility and adaptability to change;
- a wider perspective and an ability to see things from a different viewpoint.

By their very nature, many of the value-added and unintended outcomes will be challenging to measure; however, there are a number of steps that can be taken to assess these results:

Table 7.1 The usefulness of different evaluation methods to each level of Kirkpatrick's model

	Level 1 (Reaction)	**Level 2 (Learning)**	**Level 3 (Performance)**	**Level 4 (Organization)**	**Level 5 (ROI)**
Reaction sheets	High	Medium	Low	Low	Low
End tests	Low	High	Medium	Low	Medium
Post-course review	High	High	High	Medium	Medium
Completed action plans	Medium	High	High	Medium	Medium
Group discussion	High	High	High	Medium	Low
Questionnaires	High	Medium	Low	Low	Low
Structured interviews	Medium	High	High	Medium	Medium
Retesting	Low	High	Medium	Low	Low
Error rates	Low	Medium	High	High	High
Complaints	Low	Medium	High	High	High
Staff turnover	Low	Low	Medium	High	High
Staff survey	Low	Medium	Medium	Medium	Medium
Customer feedback	Low	Low	Medium	High	High
Profit levels	Low	Low	Medium	Medium	High
Financial turnover	Low	Low	Medium	High	High
Accident rates	Low	Medium	High	High	High
Wastage	Low	Medium	Medium	High	High
360-degree feedback	Low	Medium	High	High	High
Qualifications	Low	High	High	Medium	Medium
Appraisal	Medium	High	High	Medium	Low
Trend line analysis	Low	Low	High	High	High
Controls and pilots	Low	Low	High	High	High
Management information	Low	Low	High	High	High

- Encourage individual learners to reflect upon their learning and the results of development activities, not only by considering the development objectives, but also by thinking about the other impacts that the activities may have had. Reflection could be ongoing and often learners cannot identify all their gains until some time after their learning experience.
- Look for the unexpected – this may be a change in behaviour, a change in the way someone works or a change in general attitude and demeanour. These areas can be discussed effectively during appraisal meetings and ongoing review meetings.
- If you notice a difference in performance within your team, which cannot be explained, consider whether this may be a result of the learning and development activity.
- Review feedback from customers and other teams – different types or quantity of feedback may be a result of learning being implemented in unexpected/unplanned ways.

8

Putting Your Learning into Practice

Earlier in the book, we stressed the importance of reflection and planning as part of the learning process; here we provide space for you to review what you have gained from reading this book and how you will put it into practice.

What new information have I gained from this book?

What has this book reminded me about?

Which of these development methods could I use for myself? How and when?

Which of these development methods could I use for others? Who, how and when?

What other information or help do I need to make my plans work?

How will I know when and if they have been successful?

References and Further Reading

Armstrong, M (2004) *How to be an Even Better Manager: A complete A–Z of proven technique and essential skills*, 6th edn, Kogan Page, London

Armstrong, M (2006) *Human Resource Management Practice*, 10th edn, Kogan Page, London

Atherton, J S (2005a) *Learning and Teaching: Reflection and reflective practice* [Online], UK: Available: http://www.learningandteaching.info/learning/reflecti.htm

Atherton, J S (2005b) *Learning and Teaching: Critical reflection* [Online], UK: Available: http://www.learningandteaching.info/learning/critical1.htm

Beard, C and Wilson, J P (2005) *The Power of Experiential Learning: A handbook for trainers and educators*, Kogan Page, London

Berglas, S (2002) The very real dangers of executive coaching, *Harvard Business Review*, **80** (6), June, pp 86–92

Boal, A and Jackson, A (tr) (2002) *Games for Actors and Non-Actors*, Routledge, London

Boydell, T and Leary, M (1996) *Identifying Training Needs*, CIPD, London

British Learning Association website: www.british-learning.org.uk

Brockbank, A and McGill, I (2003) *The Action Learning Handbook: Powerful techniques for education, professional development and training*, Routledge Falmer, London

Brown, C L (1997) *Essential Delegation Skills* (The Smart Management Guides series) Gower Publishing Ltd, London

Cannell, M (1997) *The IPD Guide to On-the-Job Training*, CIPD, London

Caplan, J (2003) *Coaching for the Future: How smart companies use coaching and mentoring*, CIPD, London

Carter, A (2001) *Executive Coaching: Inspiring performance at work*, IES Report 379, Institute for Employment Studies, Brighton

CIPD Annual Survey Report 2006 Learning and Development: www.cipd.co.uk/surveys

CIPD: www.cipd.co.uk/elearning

Clutterbuck, D and Megginson, D (2005) How to create a coaching culture, *People Management*, **11** (8), 21 April, pp 44–45

Cunningham, I and Dawes, G (1999) *Assessing your Coaching Capability*, Topics for Trainers, CIPD, London. Available at: http://www.cipd.co.uk/subjects/lrnanddev/coachmntor/asscoach.htm

Davidson, S (2002) How to... choose the right coach. *People Management*, **8** (10), 16 May, pp 54–55

Employment Department (1971) *Glossary of Training Terms*, HMSO, London

Fincham, R and Rhodes, P (1999) *Principles of Organizational Behaviour*, Oxford University Press, Oxford

Hardingham, A, Brearley, M and Moorhouse, A (2004) *The Coach's Coach: Personal development for personal developers*, CIPD, London

Harrison, R (1997) *Employee Development*, CIPD, London

Hart, R (1996) *Effective Networking for Professional Success*, Kogan Page, London

Hawkins, P and Shohet, R (2000) *Supervision in the Helping Professions*, 2nd edn, Open University Press, Maidenhead

Hay, J (1999) *Transformational Mentoring*, Sherwood Publishing, Watford

Hogan, C (2000) *Facilitating Empowerment: A handbook for facilitators, trainers and individuals*, Kogan Page, London

Institute of Training and Occupational Learning (ITOL) (2000) *A Glossary of UK Training and Occupational Learning Terms*, ed J Brooks, ITOL, Liverpool

Jackson, T (2006) *Career Development*, CIPD factsheet, CIPD, London

Jarvis, J (2004) *Coaching and Buying Coaching Services. A guide*, CIPD, London. Available at: http://www.cipd.co.uk/guides

Keenan, K (1996) *The Management Guide to Delegating*, Ravette Publishing, Horsham

Koppett, K (2001) *Training to Imagine: Practical improvisational theatre techniques to enhance creativity, teamwork, leadership and learning*, Stylus Publishing, Sterling, VA

Koppett, K (2002) *Training Using Drama: Successful development techniques from theatre and improvisation*, Kogan Page, London

Kubicek, M (2004) Be one step ahead, *Training Magazine*, October, pp 21–23

Lamont, G (2004) *The Creative Path, Living a More Vibrant Life*, Azure, London

Learning and Skills Council, www.lsc.gov.uk

Lee, G (2004) How to buy coaching, *People Management*, **10** (5), 11 March, pp 50–51

Leigh, A and Maynard, M (2004) *Dramatic Success! Theatre techniques to transform & inspire your working life*, Nicholas Brealey Publishing, London

Leopold, J, Harris, L and Watson, T (1999) *Strategic Human Resourcing: Principles, perspectives and practices*, Financial Times Pitman Publishing, London

Mackey, D and Livsey, S (2006) *Transforming Training: A guide to creating a flexible learning environment: The rise of the learning architects*, Kogan Page, London

McGill, I and Beaty, L (2000) *Action Learning: A practitioner's guide*, Routledge Falmer, London

Misner, I R (1994) *The World's Best Known Marketing Secret: Building your business with word of mouth marketing*, Bard & Stephen, Austin, TX

Mumford, A (1995) *Effective Learning*, CIPD, London

Neill J: www.wilderdon.com

Open and Distance Learning Quality Council website: www.odlqc.org.uk

The Open University website: www.open.ac.uk

Paris, K and Mason, S (1995) *Planning and Implementing Youth Apprenticeship and Work-based Learning*, University of Wisconsin, Center on Education and Work, Madison, WI

Parsloe, E (1999) *The Manager as Coach and Mentor*, 2nd edn, CIPD, London

Pedler, M, Burgoyne, J and Boydell, T (1997) *The Learning Company*, 2nd edn, McGraw-Hill, Maidenhead

Pedler, M (1996) *Action Learning for Managers*, Lemos and Crane, London

Priest, S and Gass, M (1997) *Effective Leadership in Adventure Programming*, Human Kinetics, Champaign, IL

Proctor, B (1986) Supervision: a co-operative exercise in accountability, in *Enabling and Ensuring: Supervision in practice*, ed A Marken and N Payne, Leicester National Youth Bureau/Council for Education and Training in Youth and Community Work, Leicester

Rae, L (2001) *Develop Your Training Skills*, Kogan Page, London

Rae, L (2002) *Trainer Assessment: A Guide to measuring the performance of trainers and facilitators*, Gower, Aldershot

Rea, D G (1994a) *Evaluating Training*, Kogan Page, London

Rea, D G (1994b) *Identifying Training Needs*, Kogan Page, London

Rea, D G (1994c) *Selecting Training Methods*, Kogan Page, London

Reid, M A and Barrington, H (1999) *Training Interventions: Promoting learning opportunities*, 6th edn, CIPD, London

Revans, R W (1980) *Action Learning*, Frederick Muller Ltd, London

Rothwell, W J (1999) *Action Learning Guidebook*, Jossey-Bass/Pfeiffer, San Francisco

Sadler-Smith, E (2006) *Learning and Development for Managers: Perspectives from research and practice*, Blackwell, Oxford

Schön, D A (1983) *The Reflective Practitioner: How professionals think in action*, Temple Smith, London

Sector Skills Development Agency (SSDA) www.ssda.org.uk

Shea, G F (1992) *Mentoring: A guide to the basics*, Kogan Page, London

Sloman, M (2005) *Training to Learning. Change agenda*, CIPD, London

Smart, J K (2002) *Real Delegation: How to get people to do things for you – and do them well*, Prentice Hall, London

Smith, M K (2001) Donald Schön: learning, reflection and change, in *the encyclopedia of informal education*, www.infed.org/thinkers/et-schon.htm

Starkey, K (ed) (1996) *How Organizations Learn*, International Thomson Business Press, London

The National Recognition Information Centre for the United Kingdom (UK NARIC), www.naric.org.uk

The Qualifications and Curriculum Authority (QCA), www.qca.org.uk

The UK National Reference Point for Vocational Qualifications (UK NRP), www.uknrp.org.uk

Thorpe, S and Clifford, J (2000) *Dear Trainer: Dealing with difficult problems in training*, Kogan Page London

Thorpe, S and Clifford, J (2003) *The Coaching Handbook: An action kit for trainers and managers*, Kogan Page, London

Various contributors (2003) *Train the Trainer: The definitive guide to creating a great learning experience*, Fenman, Ely

Wade, P A (1995) *Measuring the Impact of Training*, Kogan Page, London

Weinstein, K (1998) *Action Learning: A practical guide*, Gower, Aldershot

Wilson, J R (1991) *Word of Mouth Marketing*, John Wiley & Sons, Chichester

www.clinical-supervision.com

Index

absence management (case study) 137–40
academic qualifications 82–85
case study 153–56
action learning 29–33
action learning sets 30, 31
activist 21–22
actors 48–49
see also drama-based learning
added value 163–65
adult learning 19–26
analysing learning needs
see development need, analysing
appraisal 15–16
apprenticeships 33–36
government-funded 33–34
organization-funded 34
approaches, traditional 2, 7, 147–50
approaches, developmental 1–3, 5–7, 150–51
assessing the impact 157–65
why 157–58
how 158–65
assessment (testing) 16
assessment and development centres 17
attitudes
see Bloom's taxonomy
auditory learning preference 23

blended learning 53
case study 137–40
see also e-learning
Bloom's taxonomy 19–20
budget 127–28
business plans 17

case studies
academic qualification (manager as researcher) 153–56
blending learning methods (absence management) 137–40
competency-based learning and development 129–31
leadership skills 151–53
multi-skilling staff 142–43
small business needs 140–41
team development (using NVQs) 144–46
time management skills 147–51
using vocational

qualifications 89–90
CBT (computer-based training)
see e-learning
change 5–7, 12
checklist
selecting development methods 119
preparing for distance learning 47
self-study 100
coaching
coaching 36–39
executive coaching 58–60
and mentoring 60
competency-based learning and development 129–31
conscious competence 24
conscious incompetence 24
core beliefs 1–2
critical incident analysis 16

delegation 39–43
stages of 40–41
department development plans 134, 140–46
development, definition 8
development need
analysing 11–17
definition 8
prioritization of 122
development plans 133–56
discussion boards and groups 43–45
distance learning 45–48
double-loop learning 27
drama-based learning 48–52

e-learning 52–57
asynchronous networks 52
costing 55–56
learning management systems 55
modes of 53–54
synchronous networks 52
environment 127
environmental factors 122–29
error rates and reporting 17
evaluation 160–63
different techniques 164
see also assessing the impact
executive coaching 58–60
experiential learning 20, 92
see also adult learning

government-funded apprenticeships 33–34

Honey and Mumford's learning styles 20–22

identifying needs 11–17
individual development plans 146–56
interviews 15

kinaesthetic learning preference 23
Kirkpatrick's evaluation model 158–59
knowledge
see Bloom's taxonomy
Kolb's learning cycle 20, 92

leadership skills (case study) 151–53
learning, definition of 7–8
learning and development
context 5–9
definition 8
methods 29–117
learning curve 25
learning cycle

see Kolb's learning cycle
learning, impact on organization 161
see also assessing the impact
learning management systems 55
learning methods 29–117
learning sets
see action learning
learning styles 20–23
activist 21–22
line management, responsibility for learning and development 2, 7

mentoring 60–63
methods
academic qualifications 82–85
action learning 29–33
apprenticeships 33–36
coaching 36–39
delegation 39–43
discussion boards and groups 43–45
distance learning 45–48
drama-based learning 48–52
e-learning 52–57
executive coaching 58–60
mentoring 60–63
networking 63–67
on-the-job training 67–70
organizational learning methods 116–17
outdoor education / learning 70–73
professional membership 74–76
professional supervision 77–79
projects 79–82
qualifications 82–92
reflective practice 92–96
secondments 96–99
self-study 99–101
shadowing 102–105
temporary promotion 105–107
trade exhibitions 107–109
training courses 109–16
vocational qualifications 85–92
methods, selecting 119–31
motivating adults to learn 26
multi-skilling (case study) 142–43

National Vocational Qualifications (NVQs) 85–92
needs analysis
see development need, analysing
needs, prioritizing
see development needs, prioritization of
networking 63–67

on-the-job training 67–70
open learning
see distance learning
organization's development history 125
organization's goals and objectives 124
organizational culture 123–24
organizational factors 122–29
organizational learning 27
methods of 116–17
organizational development plans 134–41
organization-funded apprenticeships 34
outcomes, clarifying 120
outdoor education/learning 70–73

peer coaching
see coaching

people resource 126
performance appraisal
  see appraisal
personal development plan
  see individual development plans
  see putting your learning into practice 167–68
personal motivation
  see motivating adults to learn
pragmatist 21–22
prioritization
  see development needs, prioritization of
professional membership 74–76
professional supervision 77–79
projects 79–82
putting your learning into practice 167–68

qualifications 82–92
quality monitoring
  see error rates and reporting
questionnaires 14–15

reflective journals 93–94
reflective practice 92–96
reflector 21–22
research (case study) 153–56
resources, available 128–29
return on investment 160–63
role play
  see drama-based learning

secondments 96–99
selecting development methods 119–31
  see also development plans
self-study 99–101
sensory learning preferences 22–23
shadowing 102–105
single-loop learning 27
sitting by Nellie
  see on-the-job training
skills
  see Bloom's taxonomy
skills matrices (case study) 142–43
stakeholders 125–26
standards 12–13
stimulus
  see how adults learn
supervision
  see professional supervision
  see line management, responsibility for learning and development

team development (case studies) 142–43, 144–46
team development plans 141–46
temporary promotion 105–107
testing 16
theorist 21–22
theory of competence 23–25
time 122
time management (case study) 147–51
trade exhibitions 107–109
training
courses 1–3, 5–7, 109–16
definition of 7
training courses 109–16

unconscious competence 25
unconscious incompetence 23
unintended outcomes 163–65

validation 159–60
  see also assessing the impact
video
  see drama-based learning
visual learning preference 23
vocational qualifications 85–92

FURTHER READING FROM KOGAN PAGE

Coaching and Mentoring, by Eric Parsloe and Monika Wray
The Essential Guide to Managing Talent, by Kaye Thorne and Andy Pellant
Excellence in Coaching, edited by Jonathan Passmore
Experiential Learning, by Colin Beard and John P Wilson
The Group Trainer's Handbook, by David Leigh
A Handbook of Human Resource Management Practice, by Michael Armstrong
A Handbook of Management and Leadership, by Michael Armstrong and Tina Stephens
A Handbook of Management Techniques, by Michael Armstrong
Human Capital Management, by Angela Baron and Michael Armstrong
Human Resource Development, by John P Wilson
Improving Employee Performance through Workplace Learning, by Earl Carter and Frank McMahon
Managing Projects in Human Resources, Training and Development, by Vivien Martin
Mentoring in Action, by David Megginson, David Clutterbuck, Bob Garvey, Paul Stokes, Ruth Garrett-Harris
Performance Management: Key Strategies and Practical Guidelines, by Michael Armstrong
The Theory and Practice of Training, by Jim Caple and Roger Buckley
The Training Design Manual, by Tony Bray
Transforming Training, by David Mackey and Sian Livsey
Strategic Human Resource Management, by Michael Armstrong
Strategic Reward: Making it Happen, by Michael Armstrong and Duncan Brown

